BEYOND THE SKY

YOU AND THE UNIVERSE

DARA Ó BRIAIN

with Kate Davies

Illustrated by Dan Bramall

D0415175

Scholastic Children's Books,
Euston House, 24 Eversholt Street,
London NW1 1DB, UK

A division of Scholastic Ltd
London ~ New York ~ Toronto ~ Sydney ~ Auckland
Mexico City ~ New Delhi ~ Hong Kong

Published in the UK by Scholastic Ltd, 2017

Text © Dara Ó Briain, 2017
Illustrations © Dan Bramall, 2017

All rights reserved

Trade hardback edition ISBN 978 1407 17899 8
Scholastic Clubs and Fairs edition ISBN 978 1407 18183 7

Printed and bound in Slovakia

2 4 6 8 10 9 7 5 3 1

The right of Dara Ó Briain and Dan Bramall to be identified as the
author and illustrator of this work respectively has been asserted by
them in accordance with the Copyright, Designs and
Patents Act, 1988.

This book is sold subject to the condition that it shall not, by
way of trade or otherwise be lent, resold, hired out, or otherwise
circulated without the publisher's prior consent in any form or
binding other than that in which it is published and without a
similar condition, including this condition, being imposed upon the
subsequent purchaser.

Papers used by Scholastic Children's Books are made from wood
grown in sustainable forests.

BEYOND THE SKY

YOU AND THE UNIVERSE

DARA Ó BRIAIN

with Kate Davies

Illustrated by Dan Bramall

■ SCHOLASTIC

This book is dedicated to O and C and N, who tirelessly explore the very limits of what they can get away with.

CONTENTS

SO YOU WANT TO GO INTO SPACE?

What? Are you mad? Why?

No, really – it's just a **terrible**, **TERRIBLE** idea. We humans are **PERFECTLY** designed for life on Earth. We can walk around, breathe, drink water, eat vegetables, read books, not get **FROZEN** or **fried** or **squished** when we go outside – it's **LOVELY**.

That **COMFY** chair you're sitting on right now? They don't have that in space. And even if they did, every time you moved around in it, you'd start **floating** away from it because there wasn't the same amount of **GRAVITY** to hold you down; and now you're kicking and flapping your hands to try to swim back to the chair and you start to get out of breath, but what's that? **THERE'S NO AIR IN SPACE!** Or at least not in the bit between the planets, and even on the planets that have some gas, which you might hopefully call 'AIR', it's not made of the same chemicals as lovely Earth air, and so we can't breathe it, so good luck with that.

This is a **DREADFUL** idea.

Even before that, when you floated out of your lovely, soft chair into the big empty S P A C E that is space, your body would swell up, and the moisture on your tongue might start to boil. You'd also probably get a nasty **sunburn** because you wouldn't have the protection we're used to here against the full **heat** of the Sun. And even if you survived all THAT, well, you're not near anything, are you? Space is mind-bogglingly, brain-fryingly **huge** and the things that are in space – **comets** and **moons** and **black holes** and **exploding stars** and all that stuff – are so far away from us and each other that it would take more time than we'll ever be alive to try to go and see them.

So what's the point?

But then again ...

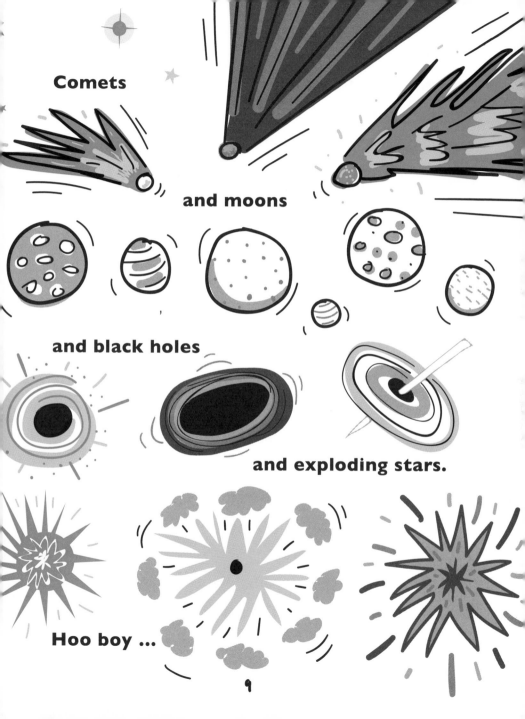

Comets

and moons

and black holes

and exploding stars.

Hoo boy ...

9

They sound pretty good. And we haven't even mentioned **asteroid belts** and **galaxies colliding** and **planets with rings around them** and **aliens** and **constellations** and **EVERYTHING**.

So some pretty great stuff there. The stuff we've been staring up at and **WONDERING** about and trying to reach out to, since, well, since the beginning of us looking up and wondering.

Okay, I can see why you want to head out and start **EXPLORING**. It's built into us as humans. People have been **DREAMING** about space travel for centuries. Lives have been lost to it, great **BRAINS** dedicated to it, the entire world captivated watching nations **race** to conquer it. There are many, myself included, who think that the journeys we've made into space are among the **GREATEST** things we've ever achieved as a species, (just pipping **indoor toilets** and **KETCHUP**).

Space must be about the astronauts, then — those lucky few that get to put on a spacesuit and sit in the capsule or **SPIN** in zero gravity. **Who knows?** You might get to be one of those yourself. So we'll see how far they've gone and just how **DIFFICULT** it was to do. (Wait until you hear about the toilets. **YIKES!**)

But, and this is a big, big **BUT**, astronauts can only take us so far. There are so many places that they can never go – places that are just too **DANGEROUS** to visit, or just so faaaaar away that the journey would take years, or where the ticket is **ONE-WAY** because there *is* no way back – and you might think, well, no exploring there, we've reached our limit, but **NO!** Because you can be the explorer who builds **rockets** and **robots** and **probes** and sends them to all corners of the Solar System, so they can tell us what they find. And we can get to know our own neighbourhood, our nearby planets and moons and asteroids that spin around our Sun.

Where's the return part?

TICKETS

Or maybe that isn't enough for you.

Maybe you want to ask the **BIGGEST QUESTIONS OF ALL.** Questions like:

* **What is this Universe we live in?**
* **How did it begin?**
* **How will it end?**
* What's out there, beyond this tiny corner of ours, with our eight measly planets?
* **What rocket will bring us those answers?**

And the answer will be **no rocket at all**, but a series of amazing time machines, operated from right here on Earth, that allow us to look further and further into the past, and get answers to these amazing questions.

You said you wanted to go exploring? Well, the Universe is out there waiting for you. **Why don't we go together and see what we can find?**

HOW FAR WE'VE BEEN

Humans haven't actually travelled very far into space at all. The furthest we've ever gone is the Moon, which is a bit like POPPING out for a bag of crisps in space-travel terms. That's because, as I've mentioned, space travel is **DANGEROUS**. It's also **expensive** – a spacesuit alone costs millions of dollars, let alone the spacecraft. And, as I feel we'll be mentioning a lot, space is **BIG** and planets and stars are really far away from each other, so it takes a really long time to get anywhere. If you travelled to Mars on the FASTEST spaceship that currently exists, it would take about **EIGHT MONTHS**. It takes so long to get there that by the time you arrived, you'd have **GROWN OUT** of your clothes. In fact, scientists think the journey to Mars would be so boring that it might be a good idea to put the astronauts into a **deep sleep** for most of the trip so that they don't go **MAD** and start **SCREAMING**, "Are we nearly there yet?" at each other twenty times an hour.

Even starting a space journey is difficult, thanks to gravity. Gravity is a **force** – forces are how things invisibly interact, and they can either *PUSH* or **PULL**. This sounds like a very complicated idea except that you've probably demonstrated this a million times, any time you've held magnets next to each other and seen them react. **Magnetism** is a force and depending on which way you hold the magnet, it can *PUSH* the other magnet away or it can **PULL** it closer.

Gravity only pulls things closer though, and you don't have to be made of some special metal like a magnet to create gravity. Every single thing with physical **MASS** (you, this book, your dinner) is pulling on everything else all the time. It's much weaker than magnetism though, which is lucky or we'd all be clumped together in **A BIG BALL** with our **dinners**, **BOOKS** and **family STUCK** to us.

When gravity starts to get really strong and important is when something has a LOT of physical mass, like this planet you're sitting on right now. Earth has a really huge gravitational pull, which you probably noticed last time you jumped and immediately got **pulled back down** to Earth.

The Earth's gravity is pulling you down towards it right now. That's why you're not floating. If you were on a planet with a smaller mass than Earth – Mars say – the gravity would be smaller and you would be able to jump higher with the same amount of effort. The Moon is pretty TITCHY, with only one sixth of Earth's mass, so astronauts were bouncing around feeling one sixth of their normal weight. Of course, if you went to a much bigger planet, its gravity would be much **STRONGER** and suddenly your legs and arms would feel much **heavier**, and walking would be twice the effort.

Wheeee!

Things with lots of gravity pull things with less mass towards them. The Earth's gravity **ATTRACTS** the Moon, which is why the Moon orbits (spins around) the Earth. The Sun's gravity pulls on the planets, which is why they orbit the Sun.

Because the Earth's gravity is so strong, spaceships need a

massive

amount of energy to **BLAST** through it and out into space. And for many years, scientists weren't sure it was possible. But back in the seventeenth century, one man predicted that humans would travel into space one day. He was **Sir Isaac Newton**, a BRILLIANT (and slightly **ECCENTRIC**) British scientist. He believed that the secret to discovering the way the Universe worked was to **OBSERVE** the world around him rather than trusting books. So he once prodded his eye with a needle to see what would happen. **GENIUS HAS ITS LIMITS.**

Very clever person

Books are great

Very stupid thing to do

Newton was also the first person to realize that gravity, the force that keeps the planets **SPINNING** around the Sun, is the same force that makes objects fall to the ground when we drop them. He said that with enough energy, a **cannonball** could break through gravity and orbit Earth. He probably didn't realize just how much energy that would be and that it would need **giant** rockets to deliver it though.

EARTH
RIGHT HERE

Officially, space starts 100 km **(60 MILES)** above our heads. Which isn't that far away. I live in London, so from my house, **SPACE** is closer than the seaside.

Wherever you live, you'll probably have travelled **FURTHER** than space to go on your holidays.

Not really that far

SPACE

THE BEACH

FAR

Travelling **100 KM** above the Earth wouldn't actually be that difficult as long as you could persuade **NASA** or the Russian Space Agency, Roscosmos, to give you a ride on one of their spaceships.

Room for a little one?

ABSOLUTELY NOT!

From there, you can gaze down at Earth from the comfort (hmm, we'll get back to this) of your gravity-free (we'll get back to this too) chamber and admire the blue-green beauty of the planet we call home.

You'll see swirling clouds and the lights from the cities below. You might see **meteors** – tiny rocks from space, burning up as they enter the Earth's atmosphere.

Lots of astronauts say that seeing our planet from space makes you feel really protective of Earth, so you'll probably end up thinking that our planet is pretty SPECIAL.

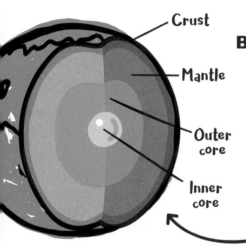

Crust

Mantle

Outer core

Inner core

EARTH: PRETTY AVERAGE

But it's not. Earth is an incredibly average planet. It's pretty much just a massive LUMP of rock, with a molten core as hot as the surface of the Sun.

Earth is in the middle of the Solar System — it's the third of the eight planets that orbit the Sun. It's not the ...

BIGGEST or SMALLEST,

or ....**FASTEST**,

or **hottest** or COLDEST planet.

It hasn't got exciting (rings) circling it, like Saturn does, and **it's only got one boring** grey moon.

Earth would be the worst planet to get if you were playing planetary Top Trumps, let's put it that way. Except that actually, **Earth's averageness** makes it very special indeed.

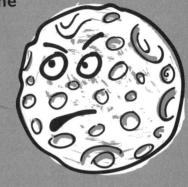

The Goldilocks zone

As far as we know, EARTH is the only planet in the SOLAR SYSTEM where life exists. And it's precisely because the Earth isn't

TOO CLOSE or **t o o F A R**

from the Sun, too **HOT** or too COLD, too **big** or too SMALL, that the conditions are **perfect** for living things to thrive.

If we were much closer to the Sun, we'd **BURN** or **fry** or **MELT** – as in: things you should only do to food.

If we were much further away, we wouldn't get enough heat from the Sun and we'd **FREEZE** – again, something you should only do to food. The human body is about 70 per cent water so we'd literally be snowmen (and women and children). And not cute ones that go on Christmas adventures with small children, either. **We'd be DEAD.**

STEP 1   STEP 2   STEP 3

But our distance from the Sun isn't the only reason there's life on Earth. There are other places more or less the same distance away that you could choose to start a species – the **MOON**, for example. It'd be pretty tough though; in the sunshine, the Moon's surface can reach over **100 °C** – hotter than **BOILING WATER**. At the same time, the part of the Moon facing away from the Sun can be as **COLD** as **-200 °C**. Coat on, coat off. Is it **FREEZING** out or **boiling?** Just checking the weather forecast would take up the whole day.

BOILING

0

FREEZING

The reason living things can survive on Earth and **not** on the Moon is because Earth has an atmosphere – a layer of gases that protects us from the Sun's **HARMFUL** rays, but also traps enough of the Sun's heat to keep us warm. The atmosphere also gives us air to breathe, which is **NICE**.

The atmosphere isn't the only reason that life thrives on Earth. We Earthlings are lucky enough to have absolutely gallons of one of the most unusual and useful substances in the Universe:

WATER.

Water is the only substance that naturally occurs on Earth in three states – **solid**, liquid and **gas**.

This is really helpful because, since water turns to gas when it gets hot and then turns back to liquid again when it cools down, it helps regulate the temperature of our planet. Water from the sea evaporates and forms **CLOUDS** and comes back down again as **RAIN**. That might not seem so helpful when the rain falls on you, but it keeps the planet at the right, toasty temperature.

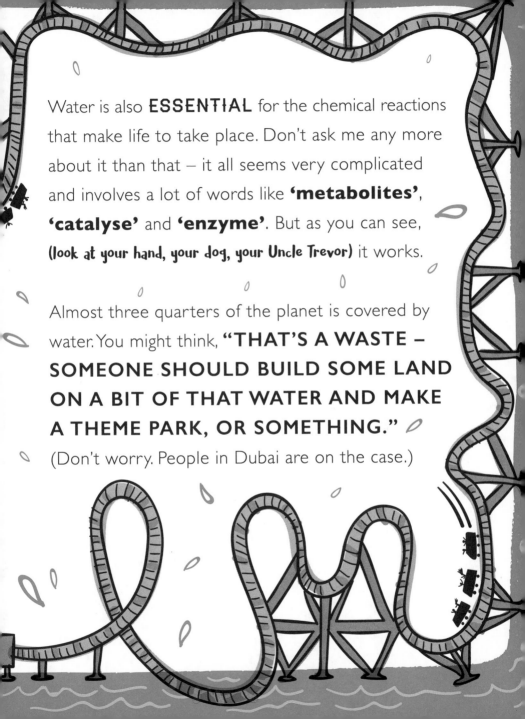

Water is also **ESSENTIAL** for the chemical reactions that make life to take place. Don't ask me any more about it than that – it all seems very complicated and involves a lot of words like **'metabolites'**, **'catalyse'** and **'enzyme'**. But as you can see, (look at your hand, your dog, your Uncle Trevor) it works.

Almost three quarters of the planet is covered by water. You might think, **"THAT'S A WASTE – SOMEONE SHOULD BUILD SOME LAND ON A BIT OF THAT WATER AND MAKE A THEME PARK, OR SOMETHING."** (Don't worry. People in Dubai are on the case.)

But without water, we'd be **STUFFED**. And we're the only planet we know to have liquid water on our surface. As far as we know (we're doing a lot of looking for water – more on this later).

The combination of all these things – atmosphere, water, just the right temperature, is what has made ordinary, medium-sized, dull little Earth the perfect place for an **EXPLOSION** of life, of plants and tigers and helicopters and country and western music and the letter **G**, and everything. And the search is on to see if we can find another planet with the same qualities, and we can meet their TIGERS and HELICOPTERS and TERRIBLE MUSIC, too.

Is there anyone out there?

We haven't found life anywhere else in the **Solar System** yet. If we did find it, it would most likely be really SMALL and SIMPLE and not playing the guitar. But there's definitely **life** out there in the **UNIVERSE** somewhere. Scientists reckon about five per cent of all the stars in the Universe could have planets with the right conditions for **life**. That might not sound like a lot, but there are something like a billion trillion stars in the Universe that we know about, so there are probably billions of **EARTH-LIKE** planets out there somewhere. In fact, in 2017 NASA discovered a whole new system of planets, around the star TRAPPIST-1, with not one, but **THREE** planets that might be just right. **See?**

Earth isn't that special after all.

THE INTERNATIONAL SPACE STATION

If you manage to hitch a ride on that **SPACESHIP**, your destination will probably be the International Space Station (ISS), a spacecraft the size of an American football field that orbits the Earth at **27,500 kilometres an hour** (km/h), or 17,080 mph.

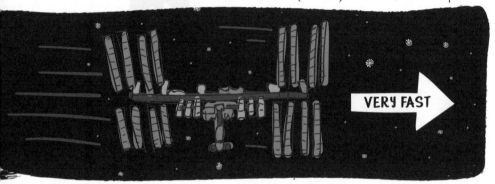

VERY FAST

Apart from its size and the fact that it's often full of Americans wearing helmets, the **ISS** has very little else in common with an American football field. It's actually a **M A S S I V E** SPACE **LABORATORY**, used by astronauts from all over the world. Over **200 people** from **five continents** have visited it –

astronauts, scientists and a few **SPACE TOURISTS** too, who were willing to pay about **$30 MILLION** each for a week's holiday in space.

We've got a lovely view from our room, but the food was much better in France

'Proper' astronauts usually stay on the ISS for about six months, though some of them stay longer (the record is a **437-day** stay, set by Russian cosmonaut, **Valerie Polyakov**, on the Russian space station, Mir). If you came to this book wanting to learn how to be a space explorer, then being a **'proper'** astronaut is probably what you were thinking of. After all, astronauts are officially the **COOLEST** people on the planet. I've met a few of them now and there is no story you can tell them they can't top, usually because they did the same thing, but in …

SPACE.

Like, "I saw the Grand Canyon once."

"Oh really, because I saw it … from **SPACE!**"

Or, "I had a lovely meal last night."

"Yep, so did I … in **SPACE!**"

Actually, forget that, astronauts are a pain. And besides, living as an astronaut is often a pain, too.

Life on the ISS is very different to Earth. Most of the ISS is made up of solar panels, and the part the astronauts actually live in is about the size of a five-bedroom house, with six of you sharing, and you can't go outside without a spacesuit, so it gets pretty CLAUSTROPHOBIC.

There's no gravity, so you **FLOAT** around a lot. Floating around is quite confusing to the brain, so a lot of astronauts get space sick when they start, which is like getting seasick but **WORSE**, because your vomit just floats around the spaceship afterwards and is a real pain to clean up. It costs so much money to transport water to space that you can't have a shower – you use a **WET-WIPE** to mop your armpits and hope for the best. NASA used to do tests on astronauts to see how long they could go without washing at all. **Exciting news!** Eventually your nose stops telling you how smelly it is, but not for about **eight days**. Even if you *could* have a shower, the water would float in the air and you'd have to **DANCE** around after it and would look a bit **FOOLISH**.

ZZZZZ

Because liquid floats in space, you have to **SUCK** drinks from plastic bags and watch out for **DRIPS** in case they float into the computers. Because *humans* **float** in space, you have to sleep in a sleeping bag tied to the wall, and exercise for two hours a day to stop your legs and bones wasting away. It's difficult to **BURP** in space because the air bubbles don't travel upwards like they do on Earth. And then there's the whole terrible **going to the toilet** business. One word: **SUCTION**. And in case you were wondering, the wee gets recycled, filtered and turned back into drinking water. The **POO** gets bagged and sent back to Earth.

What did you bring me back from space, Daddy?

Ah, not sure you'll like it ...

The astronauts on the ISS don't spend all their time floating around, exercising and feeling **CLAUSTROPHOBIC,** though. They do experiments to study things like how space travel affects the human body. Spoiler: space travel affects the human body **BADLY**. It's the lack of **gravity**. We don't even notice it here on Earth but it's like we're constantly in a gym lifting **weights**, just carrying ourselves around while gravity is trying to pull us down. Take away that **gravity** and the muscles and bones quickly start to get weaker and weaker. Even with two hours' exercise a day, when

astronauts return to Earth they are often so weak in normal **gravity** that they can hardly walk.

A quick note about zero gravity though, and then I promise to stop mentioning **GRAVITY**, at least for a page or two. A lot of people seem to think that astronauts on the ISS float around in zero G because they are so high above the Earth that the **GRAVITY** can't get them. Ask the next grown-up you meet if they think this, and if they say yes, slowly shake your head as if to say, **"I'm very disappointed in you."**

The ISS is only about 400 km, or 250 miles, above us and there is **LOADS OF GRAVITY** up there. If you found a ladder that was 400 km long, climbed to the top and stepped off, you wouldn't float around. You'd start falling really, really quickly back down to Earth.

Let's explain it this way. Have you noticed when you're in a lift that starts going down and

just for a second you feel a little LIGHTER? Well, if that lift just dropped without anything slowing it (this is called freefall), you'd feel completely **WEIGHTLESS**, at least until the small bump where it hit the ground. Basically the ISS and all satellites in **orbit** are in freefall, but in a sideways path that keeps them spinning around the Earth, rather than **PLUMMETING** towards it. That's why they travel at 27,500 KM/H, or 17,500 MPH, it's the speed they need to keep just missing the Earth and stay in **orbit**.

Do you know in museums where they have that **STRANGE SHAPE** you can **ROLL** coins into, and watch them go round and round and slowly DISAPPEAR into the middle? Well gravity is like that big **HOLE** in the middle and an orbit is like the coin spinning **ENDLESSLY** round the lip of the **HOLE**. If you **don't** know that thing in museums where the coin spins around a strange shape until it disappears down the middle, well, this comparison didn't help at all.

There are **COOL** things about going to the **ISS** too. The space station orbits the Earth once every 90 minutes, so you'll see sixteen sunsets and sixteen sunrises a day. Once you get over the **space-sickness**, zero G becomes a lot of fun, and handy too. Astronauts are well known, when they return to Earth, to **DROP** things like pens and cups and computers in mid-air just because they are so used to having them f l o a t wherever they leave them.

If you're really lucky you might have put on a special suit and do an **EVA**, an **Extra-vehicular activity**, more commonly known as a **SPACEWALK**. And if you're really **LUCKY** you'll get a few minutes outside to just watch the Earth and everyone you've ever known, roll by beneath you.

Plus there is **one room** in the ISS that is just big enough to carry an astronaut in and then

leave him floating, just out of reach of any walls or handholds and they'll be stuck there flapping round until you rescue them.

Sign me up!

If you fancy a trip to the ISS, then the easiest thing to do is become a **BILLIONAIRE** and pay **$40 million** for the privilege. If you'd rather do it the CHEAP way, you'll have to become an astronaut. **TO DO THAT, YOU NEED TO**:

1 Learn Russian. Most **SPACESHIPS** are **Russian**, and all the instructions on the controls are Russian, and most of the other people in space are Russian, so you'll be **STUCK** if you don't.

2 Learn to swim: when you leave the ISS, you'll probably crash-land back on Earth in the middle of the sea. Maybe take one of those whistles from aeroplane life jackets, too, in case you need to attract **ATTENTION**.

Toot toot

42

3 Learn to survive in the wilderness
– if you don't land in the sea, you'll probably land in the middle of a FREEZING forest in Siberia and have to fight off **WOLVES**.

4 Get a degree in science and maths. You'll be doing **experiments** in space – and you'll need to plot the course of spaceships and probes to make sure they get to the right place at the right time. Lots of people want to be **ASTRONAUTS**, so make sure you get better marks than everyone else.

Don't go too far

5 Learn to fly a jet plane – it's a lot like flying a spaceship, apparently.

LOW EARTH ORBIT
– 180 TO 2,000 KM ABOVE EARTH

The **ISS** orbits the Earth at '**LOW EARTH ORBIT**', which means it's not that far away from the planet's surface. If going to the Moon is the space equivalent of only going as far as the corner shop, Low Earth orbit is the space equivalent of stepping on to the doorstep to see if you need a coat.

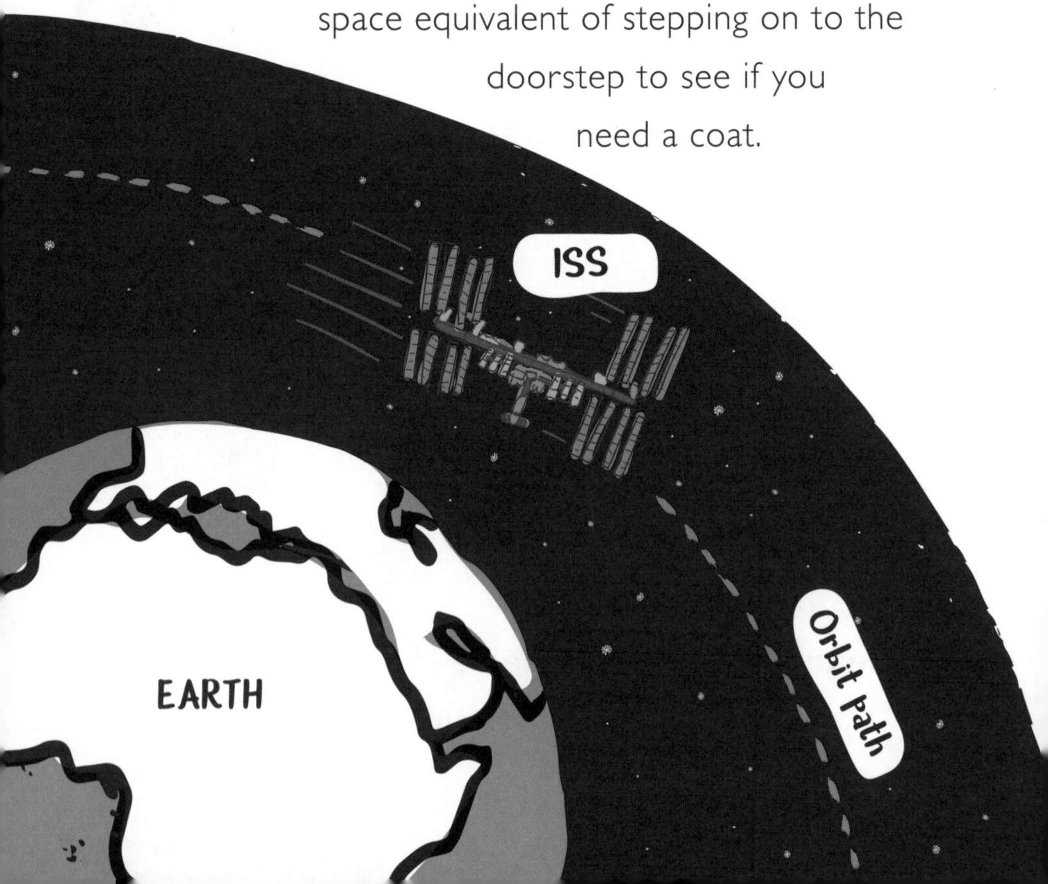

ISS

EARTH

Orbit Path

It's also the part of the part of space we've put the most stuff in. Between where the ISS **ORBITS**, (about 400 km up) and the farthest out orbits (about 36,000 km away) there are over **4,000** satellites *FLOATING* around, although it is thought that only about a third of these are **still working.**

Satellites are the man-made machines that humans put in space to send and receive SIGNALS from Earth. There are all kinds of satellites orbiting the Earth – mobile phone satellites, which allow us to talk instantly to people on the other side of the planet; television satellites, without which your TV might go **crackly** when you're watching the football; Global Positioning

System satellites that tell us whether to turn left or right; and **SPY** satellites, without which enemy countries wouldn't be able to spy on each other illegally.

SPY SATELLITE

In fact, it's **AMAZING** how often, and unnoticeably, we use these spacecraft day-to-day without even thinking about it. Spare a thought though, next time you're watching the football on a satellite channel, for the poor commentators who have to fly up to the satellite to present the show.

That's not true by the way, but I bet you could make somebody believe it if you said it with a straight face. **Try it on your dad.**

The Hubble Telescope

If you twisted my arm and **forced** me to pick my favourite artificial satellite, I'd choose the Hubble Space Telescope. It's a telescope ... and it's in space!

FANTASTIC.

Hubble is no ordinary telescope. In fact, it's one of the most **BRILLIANT** scientific inventions in history.

I'm one of the most important inventions in history

HUBBLE: NOT HUMBLE

The reason Hubble is so brilliant is that it can take photos of space from outside the Earth's atmosphere. The atmosphere is very useful if you want to breathe and stay alive and all that, but it's **terrible** if you want to get a good, clear look at a star. You know how the stars look a bit

Twinkle, twinkle, little star...

blurry and twinkly when you look up at them? That's the atmosphere getting in the way. **NEVER** sing *Twinkle, Twinkle, Little Star* to a professional astronomer to get them to sleep. They **HATE** twinkle. They'll just get all **TENSE** and won't be able to sleep for ages.

Hubble was the first big, **POWERFUL** telescope in space. It was launched in 1990, and everyone was very **EXCITED** about seeing the first clear pictures of our galaxy and the rest of the Universe.

UNFORTUNATELY, the pictures Hubble sent back to Earth weren't actually that clear at all. They were a *bit* clearer than the pictures telescopes could take from Earth, but it still looked as if someone had jogged Hubble's elbow a bit as it was taking them. Hubble doesn't have an elbow, so scientists could immediately rule that out as the source of the problem. Eventually they figured out that one of the mirrors in the telescope was slightly the wrong shape, which was a bit of a shame, as the whole thing had cost **$1.5 billion** to make.

A lot of people thought Hubble was a **DISASTER**. It was the laughing stock of the telescope community for a while. But in 1993, the clever people at NASA sent astronauts up to fix it. The repairs involved five EVAs – trips outside the safety of the spaceship into the terrifying emptiness of space – but the astronauts

HA

HA HA

pulled it off. Since then, Hubble has taken incredibly clear, **beautiful** photographs of the Universe that have led to all kinds of amazing discoveries. Information from Hubble has helped scientists figure out the age of the Universe (about 13.7 billion years), and the fact that the expansion of the Universe is *SPEEDING UP* rather than slowing down as scientists had previously thought. Thanks to Hubble and the astronomers and scientists who use the telescope, we know more about the Universe we live in than ever before.

Edwin Hubble – another very clever person

The Hubble space telescope is named after an extremely cool American astronomer named **Edwin Hubble**. He proved that the blurry patches of light in the night sky were actually distant galaxies and that the Universe was **much, much bigger** than previously thought. He was also the person who proved that the Universe is EXPANDING – getting bigger and more spread out all the time (we'll get back to this). And he did all of that by looking up at the sky through a blurry telescope from Earth. Who knows what he'd have discovered if he'd been **alive** when the Hubble space telescope was launched? Plus, since they named it after him, he'd definitely have been given the first go.

THE MOON
384,400 KM ABOVE EARTH – 1.3 LIGHT SECONDS ...

Whoa! Where did this **'LIGHT SECOND'** come from? Well, when the distances begin to get pretty big, as distances in space tend to do, it's nice to deal with smaller numbers rather than trying to compare **342,817,693,124,867,924,586,794,679 km** to **327,872,341,768,123,467 km**. So, we'll start talking about distances in term of how long it takes light to travel them. Light is the *FASTEST* thing in the Universe and also always travels through space at the same speed, so it's a good benchmark. The Moon is only a **second** away for a particle of light, although the journey took just over two days when we last sent astronauts up there.

The Moon is the **FARTHEST** human beings have ever travelled in space and we haven't done it often, or recently. Only twelve people have ever walked on the Moon's surface. Their footprints are still there – there isn't any wind or rain (or any vacuum cleaners) to clean them up.

The Moon is made of the Earth itself. Scientists think it was formed when a massive object (probably about the size of Mars, so much **bigger** than any comet or asteroid) collided with the Earth about

I win! See you in a couple of days

4.5 billion years ago. The Earth was very young at the time – maybe as young as **20 million years**, which is barely a teenager in Universe terms. (Maybe it was playing music too **LOUDLY** and one of the other planets threw something at it to make it **STOP**.) When the massive object hit the Earth, bits of the Earth **FLEW OFF** and **EVENTUALLY** joined together to form the Moon.

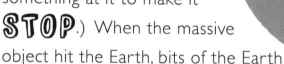

The Earth's **gravity** keeps the Moon in orbit – and the Moon's gravity pulls on the Earth, too. We can see the effect it has on us twice a day when the tides **come in** and **go out**. The Moon pulls the seas on Earth towards it, causing the water to bulge on the nearest side. And because the Earth is spinning, the water also **BULGES** on the other side, but away from the Moon. This causes the tides.

All this **ENERGY** spent on lifting our seas up and down comes at a cost though. The Earth's rotation is slowing down and, at the same time, the Moon is being pushed further away from us. You and I won't see the effects of this but, over time, they add up. When the Earth and Moon were formed, **4.5 billion years ago**, the average day was far shorter, possibly as short as just four hours. The Moon has **SLOWED** that to the more **relaxed** 24 hours we have today. If it wasn't for the Moon, we'd go to bed on **SUNDAY** night, wake up on **Tuesday**, get home from school on **WEDNESDAY**, do our homework and eventually get back to bed on **Thursday**.

The Moon moving away from us will ruin one of the great cosmic coincidences too. The Moon is about **400** times SMALLER than the Sun, but the Sun is about **400** times *FURTHER* away. This means that we (who live on Earth right now) occasionally get to see a

TOTAL LUNAR ECLIPSE,

where the Moon passes in front of the Sun and blocks it out completely. These are rare and spectacular and, if you're a bird, really, really confusing. The birds all think NIGHT HAS FALLEN and stop singing and return to

the trees. It's a
strange sort of silence
only interrupted by
humans (who understand
what's happening, hopefully)
jumping up and down with
EXCITEMENT.
Then, two minutes later, the eclipse
passes, the humans calm down
and the birds get an unexpected
wake up call. As the Moon SLOWLY
moves away from Earth this event
will DISAPPEAR
forever, sadly for us, and much to
the RELIEF of the birds.

The Moon is Earth's only
natural satellite – it orbits
the Earth once every
27.3 days. It also takes

exactly the same amount of time for the Moon to spin around itself, so we only ever see one side of it. Unlike the Sun, the Moon doesn't give off its own light – it **REFLECTS** the Sun's light to Earth, like a big, not-very-shiny mirror. The Moon looks different from Earth depending on how much sunlight is shining on it.

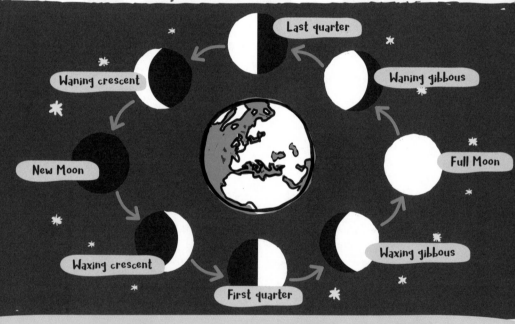

Last quarter

Waning gibbous

Waning crescent

Full Moon

New Moon

Waxing gibbous

Waxing crescent

First quarter

(This pattern is mirrored in the southern hemisphere)

So there's plenty of interesting things happening with our moon, but despite all that, we haven't been there since 1972. Scientists now usually send machines to look around for us, either as orbiters or what are charmingly called **'impactors'**, which means that they **slam** into the surface. Many cool things have happened since, like rockets now coming from **INDIA, CHINA, JAPAN** and **EUROPE**; NASA's **Lunar Reconnaissance orbiter** taking photos of the landing sites of the manned missions (even the famous footsteps!) and, when a vial of his ashes was sent up on NASA's Lunar Prospector, Eugene Shoemaker becoming the first person to be **BURIED** on the Moon – well, a bit of him at least.

Not a real tombstone ←

EUGENE SHOEMAKER

Despite that, it does feel like the time to be really **EXCITED** about the Moon was about **50 years ago ...**

The Space Race

Boy, people were **DESPERATE** to get to the Moon in the 1960s. The Soviet Union (which is now **RUSSIA**) and the United States (still the United States) absolutely **hated** each other at the time. They didn't want to go to war though, because everyone had been put off by the **Second World War,** in which around 70 million people died. Plus both countries had **NUCLEAR WEAPONS** that could kill millions of people in seconds and are generally an extremely **BAD IDEA**. Instead, the United States and the Soviet Union competed against each other to see who could invent and stockpile the

BIGGEST
MOST DESTRUCTIVE

weapons, even though they weren't planning to use them. This was called the **Cold War**, and it was the international equivalent of kids in a playground telling each other **"My brother's bigger than yours."**

My stockpile of pointless nuclear weapons is bigger than yours!

Thankfully, the two nations eventually turned their attention to **SPACE**. In 1955, the USA announced that they were going to send a **ROCKET** into space by 1958. The Soviet Union responded, **"Oh yeah? We're going to do it before you,"** but in Russian, so it sounded more **EXCITING**. And the Soviet Union *did* get there first. They launched the first artificial satellite,

SPUTNIK 1, into space on **4 October 1957**. Sputnik was the size of a beach ball, but wouldn't have been much good for throwing around by the seaside – it **weighed** about as much as I do and the four long antennae would have got in the way.

Sputnik: spiky

The Soviet Union got to the Moon **FIRST** as well, 'impacting' **Luna 2** on the surface in September 1959. The following month, **Luna 3** took the first ever photos of the far side of the Moon, a sight never before seen by human eyes.

The Soviet Union even beat the USA in sending the first human into space, too — **Yuri Gagarin** completed an orbit of the Earth on 12 April 1961. He was chosen for the mission because not only was he was good at flying planes; he was also small enough to fit in the cockpit of the spaceship — he was only 1.57 METRES, OR 5 FEET 2 INCHES, TALL.

Yuri Gagarin: tiny

One Small Step for (a) Man

Of course, the Americans were also trying their damnedest to get to the Moon as well. More than **70 separate missions** were sent to the Moon by Russia and the USA between **1958 and 1969**. As the world watched, the superpowers took turns, with launches almost once a month as the decade closed.

Slowly the Americans edged ahead. Even though they only managed to impact the Moon in 1964, **five years after the Russians**, by 1967 they had sent five successful orbiters to circle the Moon and their first successful, unmanned, lander. Russia was delayed by repeated launch failures of the ships they wanted to send as manned missions, although in **1968** they sent two TORTOISES around the Moon as a demonstration and even got them back to Earth. Three months later, the Americans sent three men to make the same trip on **Apollo 8**. They were getting closer.

In May of 1969, **Apollo 10** made the **FINAL** practice run. It was flown all the way to the Moon, descending to within 16 kilometres of the surface, and then home again. Spare a thought here for **Thomas P. Stafford**, Mission Commander on Apollo 10. He flew with two others on that trip, but they both got the chance to return to the Moon and finish the journey – John Young on Apollo 16 and Eugene Cernan on Apollo 17. Only Stafford got to get within TOUCHING DISTANCE and then had to turn around and go home. Despite the

S L O W start then, it was the USA that won the greatest prize in the **Space Race** – a manned mission to the Moon. All rehearsals over, on **21 July 1969**, Apollo 11 touched down on the Moon's surface and **Neil Armstrong** became the FIRST PERSON to set foot on a celestial body other than our own. As he **STEPPED** onto the Moon's surface, he said,

"That's one small step for man, one giant leap for mankind."

Lots of people say he muddled the words up – it was supposed to be, 'one small step for *a* man' – but Armstrong always insisted he got it right, and frankly, I think we should give him the benefit of the doubt. He was the first human being **EVER** to set foot on the Moon. Who knows what could have happened? It could have **POPPED** when he touched it. It could have been made of **CHEESE**. It could have been a giant celestial booby trap set by aliens with a cruel sense of humour. Luckily, it turned out to be a massive, empty, dusty lump of rock, just as we expected. Neil Armstrong's fellow astronaut, Buzz Aldrin, joined him on the Moon's surface soon afterwards and described it as **"magnificent desolation."**

The two men spent a few hours **BOUNCING** around the Moon's surface, taking photos of each other and doing experiments. They also planted an American flag just to annoy the Soviet Union that they'd got there first. They slept on the Moon, too, although Neil Armstrong found it hard to drift off because the **EARTHLIGHT** was so bright – the Earth reflects the Sun's light to the Moon, just as the Moon reflects sunlight to Earth. Meanwhile, the third member of the Apollo 11 crew, Michael Collins, didn't get to walk on the surface. He had to **drive** the spaceship around and around the Moon, waiting until the others were ready to come home, like an **IMPATIENT PARENT** who can't find a parking space.

While they had been getting ready to lift-off from the Moon, Buzz had noticed that in the preparation for the moonwalk, a switch had been broken off from the control panel. Without this switch the engine wouldn't start and they would have been stranded on the Moon **FOR EVER**. They radioed back to base to tell them of the problem and were told to get some sleep while a solution was found. This might be another reason why Neil Armstrong didn't get much sleep on the Moon. When they woke, NASA had no solution to the problem, so it was left to Buzz Aldrin to invent an answer. He took a **felt-tip marker pen** he had in his suit and rammed it into the hole where the switch had been. It was enough to let the engine start and they took off, re-united with Collins for the two-day journey back to Earth. (Buzz still has the pen, and the broken switch.)

When the Apollo 11 crew made it back to Earth, they were kept in **QUARANTINE** for three weeks in case they had caught diseases from the Moon. They met

US President Nixon, but they couldn't shake his hand because they were inside a specially built trailer.

You've got the lurgy

Apparently, keeping the astronauts in quarantine was a complete **WASTE OF TIME** though – they saw a trail of **ants** inside their trailer and if they could get in, any Moon bacteria would probably have got out. And there aren't any bacteria on the Moon anyway.

So, it was an eight-day trip, the culmination of years of intense work, and they spend a grand total of **two and a half hours** on the surface of the **MOON**.

Five more Apollo missions made it to the Moon, spending LONGER and LONGER on the surface each time. They drove a **moon-buggy**, hit a few **golf balls**, collected **moon-rock samples** to bring back and took many, many PHOTOGRAPHS. By Apollo 18, however, NASA budgets had been **CUT**, missions 18, 19 and 20 were **cancelled** and there hasn't been a manned mission since.

BEATEN to the ultimate prize, the Russians launched a few attempts to land an unmanned mission to extract Moon rock samples, but the last of those was in **1976** and they've **NEVER** gone back to the Moon in any form since then.

So will we ever go back? Well, don't get **disheartened** by how this all happened **50 years ago**. We seem to be ready to start that race again, and just in time for **YOU** to take part. What age will you be in 2025? That's when space agencies in Europe, Japan and China have all said they propose

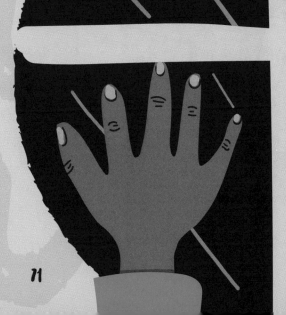

a **MANNED MISSION**. The USA want to put a manned orbiter up in **2023** and even the Russians are tentatively considering a mission by **2030**.

And it's not just countries competing now either. There's a **$20 MILLION PRIZE** for anyone who can launch a robot onto the surface of the Moon, have it travel 500 yards (that's about 457 metres) and **send pictures home**. We'll see in the next chapter how building robots will be the way to see more **INCREDIBLE** sights than astronauts ever can.

WISH YOU WERE HERE

After all, if you do get to the Moon all you have to look forward to is 'magnificent desolation'. And all the rubbish the Apollo astronauts left behind, of course. The next astronauts who land on the Moon will find **six American flags**, ONE FAMILY PHOTOGRAPH, 12 PAIRS OF SPACE BOOTS, **RAZORS**, tubes of shaving cream, **three golf balls** and around 100 bags of VOMIT, WEE and POO.

HOW FAR WE'VE SENT STUFF

So, there's the limit for astronauts, for the time being anyway. No human has travelled further than the Moon. And there are good reasons why they might **NEVER** travel further than the Moon. The D I S T A N C E, for a start. There's quite the difference between the three-day flight the Apollo astronauts made and an eight-month one, and that would only get you to Mars. You'll set up camp, have a look around, grab some rock samples, and then spend as long flying back; so you're looking at, minimum, a **YEAR-AND-A-HALF ROUND TRIP** if you want to have a proper look around.

We've sent astronauts up to the ISS for more than a year, but at least if they run out of food, we can send a rocket up with **fresh bread** and some **KitKats**. They're only 400 KM away.

If you're travelling to Mars, you have to do your

'BIG SHOP'

before you leave, and take it all with you.

Make a list of all the things you should bring on this trip. You started with food, right? Everyone starts with food. So let's pack two years of **ready meals**, those astronaut pouches we all think of when somebody says **'SPACE FOOD'**, and include enough so that they can still exercise two hours a day and not be starving all the time. Two years would be a long time without any fresh fruit or vegetables though. It would be great if we could grow food to eat as we travelled, but that is proving a **DIFFICULT CHALLENGE**.

We've been going into space for more than 50 years and we've only just recently learned how to grow things at all; in **2015** astronauts on the ISS tucked in to some leaves of **romaine lettuce** they had grown on-board. The aim is now to add **tomatoes** and **peppers**. So there's always that to look forward to. **SOME SALAD**.

And even if we solve the problem of how to keep a group of astronauts in **ham sandwiches**, the nearby destinations aren't exactly hospitable.

We have seven planets to visit in our system. Most are **FREEZING COLD**, one is **ROASTING HOT** and another is both at the same time. One has **SULPHURIC ACID** dropping as rain, which would melt the spaceship before it even landed. Most would **CRUSH** any landing craft like a tin can as it descended. And you can't **BREATHE** on any of them.

But no! We are explorers, remember? We want to see these places, **poisonous**, **CRUSHING** and **INHOSPITABLE** though they are. We are humans and we are **curious!** This is our backyard and we should be **playing** in it! So what is our solution, we ingenious humans?

We build **robots!** We build **space probes!** And we make them **EXPLORE** instead.

Robots can explore planets we couldn't physically survive going to, such as **VENUS** and **JUPITER**, with their **POISONOUS GASES**, ACID RAIN and SUFFOCATING PRESSURE. Unmanned probes can explore places too far away for humans to reach – space probes don't get old or cold or thirsty or miss their families. And they **DON'T COMPLAIN** about having to eat the same meals over and over again.

Actually, cancel that – I'm not hungry

We've come a long way since **Sputnik 1** circled the Earth for three months before running out of power. Now these machines can send back **DATA** and **PHOTOGRAPHS** for decades after they've been launched – and we can control them remotely from Earth, too, so we can see what they're **seeing** and tell them where to go and what to do.

Make it do a wheelie again

Space probes don't mind making a five-year journey to a distant planet, just to fly past it at **56,000 km/h** taking photographs. We would find that very irritating. Imagine if your holidays involved sitting on a plane for twelve hours until your Dad shouted, "Look! There's our hotel!" and you had to take pictures of it through the window as you flew by and kept going. So much of space exploration is like that. Sleep for years, take loads of photos, send them back and fly on. Sometimes flying for a very, very long time. Voyager 2 is still going, **40 years** into its journey.

Humans – they've got no stamina

So, let's hail the robots and probes and unmanned space craft that have been sent all over our Solar System. And let's applaud the **BRILLIANT** human explorers building engines that bounce us from asteroid to asteroid; who dropped a remote-controlled car by parachute onto Mars; or who landed on a comet travelling at *135,000 km/h*. And let's travel with them and see what we've learnt, playing in our own backyard.

THE SOLAR SYSTEM

Did you ever write your address like this?

JAMES BROOKS
21 HOPE STREET
BIRMINGHAM
ENGLAND
UK
EUROPE
EARTH

If so, the next line on your universal address would be:

THE SOLAR SYSTEM

The SOLAR SYSTEM is made up of the **Sun**, the **eight planets** that orbit it, the many **moons** that orbit the planets, and **asteroids** and COMETS that wait at the edges for an excuse to come hurtling past.

Before we go **EXPLORING**, some definitions will be useful. Some things we might take for granted will change from planet to planet. The word **'year'** for example. We both know that a **'year'** is the STUPIDLY LONG amount of time between when you get lots of **presents** and a CAKE with candles to blow out, and the next time you get lots of presents and a cake. And a **'day'** is actually the amount of time you would HAPPILY leave between BRUSHING your teeth because it's not like you've been eating sweets while you were asleep, so why do we have to do it in the morning as well?

But there are, surprisingly, more technical descriptions than that.

A **year** is the length of time a planet takes to **orbit** the Sun once, but planets are also spinning while they make that long journey. A **day** is the amount of time a planet takes to do one full spin.

It takes Earth 365.25 days to orbit the Sun: one year.

It takes Earth just under 24 hours to do one full spin: one day.

The **further** out we go, the **longer** the journey around the Sun, so the **longer** the year gets. The days are a real mix, but usually not far off an **Earth day**, with one glorious weird situation. Let's see if you spot it.

Here's a lovely picture of the **SOLAR SYSTEM** we call home. It's **not to scale**. If it was, the Sun would take up both pages in this book and the Earth would be the size of a full stop, somewhere down the street. We'll have a quick look at planets, with **days** and **year** and a brief list of all the **EXCITING** things they have that would instantly kill you.

THE SUN: really, really **HOT**.

MERCURY: small. Hot on one side, really cold on the other. Not very nice, and really difficult to get to without crashing into the Sun. See above for why this would be a very bad thing.
YEAR: 88 Earth days **DAY**: 59 Earth days **MOONS**: none

VENUS: pretty but deadly. Super-hot, the hottest of the lot, plus acid rain and general horribleness. Unlike most of the other planets (including us!), Venus doesn't spin in the same direction it rotates around the Sun. **YEAR**: 225 Earth days **DAY**: 243 Earth days – wait, what?! The day is **LONGER** than the year. On Venus, you have a birthday **EVERY** day! That's the only good thing about Venus. **MOONS**: none

EARTH: home
YEAR: 365.25 days
DAY: 23 hours, 56 minutes, 4 seconds **MOONS**: one

MARS: red. The planet most like Earth. But no oxygen, so don't take a deep breath. **YEAR**: 687 Earth days **DAY**: 24 hours, 37 mins **MOONS**: two

86

NEPTUNE: very blue. Extremely cold. **BR-RRRR** cold. Two scarves and a hat at least. **YEAR**: 165 Earth years. **DAY**: 16 hours, 7 minutes. **MOONS**: 13 confirmed with one very dim one waiting to be confirmed

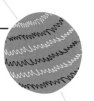

URANUS: cold and windy and lonely. Uniquely it spins on its side as it travels, a bit like a ball rolling across a floor. **YEAR**: 84 Earth years **DAY**: 17 hours, 54 minutes **MOONS**: 27

SATURN: amazing rings. Don't try to land on it, though **YEAR**: 29.5 Earth years **DAY**: 10 hours, 33 minutes **MOONS**: 53 confirmed with nine extras possible

JUPITER: big and stormy, and you'd be a pancake long before you got to the middle. **YEAR**: 12 Earth years **DAY**: 9 hours, 50 minutes. **MOONS**: as many as 67, possibly more (greedy)

Why don't the planets crash into the Sun?

A fair question, thank you for asking. It's just like when we saw the ISS **SPINNING** around Earth, constantly **FALLING**, both down and sideways, like a **coin** in that thing in the museum with the small hole in the middle, which if it has a name, **no one can remember it**.

As ever, it's all to do with **GRAVITY.** The Sun is **MASSIVE** and all that **MASS** means it creates a huge **CURVED DENT** in space for other things to **spin** around. The planets **orbit** around it just like the ISS and the Moon orbit Earth. And a **GOOD** thing they do, too, especially for us. The Sun is basically the **ONLY REASON** we're here.

THE SUN
EIGHT LIGHT MINUTES FROM EARTH
– ABOUT 149.6 MILLION KM
(93 MILLION MILES)

The Sun is eight light minutes from Earth. As we mentioned earlier, light travels through space at a constant **SPEED**, so it's a good measure of the ridiculously **huge** DISTANCES of space. It also means that the light we see from the Sun **(DON'T LOOK DIRECTLY AT THE SUN!)** left eight minutes ago, so the Sun could have completely disappeared seven minutes ago and you wouldn't know anything about it for another minute. That probably hasn't happened though. When the Sun dies, which it definitely will do in about five billion years or so, it'll **CRUNCH** the Earth up into **NOTHING**, like a massive yellow child eating a Rice Krispie. And even when the Sun burns out, it will keep shining for a million years – that's how much energy it has.

Our local star

The Sun is a **STAR**, just like all those other dots in the sky. Only this is our star and we're pressed right up against it, so it lights up the whole sky (DON'T LOOK DIRECTLY AT THE SUN! – seriously – it would really badly damage your eyes). It is also, pretty much, the source of all the energy we've ever used on the planet. Not just the heat you can feel on your face, or what we take from solar panels, but also indirectly through **PLANTS**. Plants discovered long ago how to turn sunlight into fuel for growing. Then we eat the plants, or we eat the things that ate the plants, and we get the **ENERGY.**

Or, the plants and animals die and get slowly SQUISHED down and turned into **oil**, or **gas** or **coal**, and we dig them up and burn them and get the energy. Ultimately, it's all thanks to the **SUN** – it's the only reason we're here, because you can't have life without energy. So we should thank the Sun for crisps and cartoons and video games and everything else we enjoy. Just don't say it to its face **(NEVER LOOK DIRECTLY AT THE SUN!)**.

However, though they may only be dots to us, most of the stars you see in the sky are at least as big as our Sun. Some of them are much, much bigger. **The Sun is a pretty average sort of star.** It's a 4.5 billion-year-old yellow dwarf star.

And even though the Sun is quite small for a star, it's still literally massive. It contains 99.8 per cent of the mass of the **WHOLE Solar System**. You could fit 1.3 million Earths **INSIDE** the Sun, though I don't know why you'd want to.

So many crispy treats

Earth crispies

The Sun looks perfectly round and perfectly yellow from Earth, but it's not – it's **BUMPY** and **SPOTTY** and **very, very HOT**. The coolest part of the Sun is the surface and even that is about **5,500 °C**. At its core, the temperature is about 15 million °C. It's a ball of **BURNING** gas, held together by its own gravity, and **super-tornadoes** are constantly raging on its surface – **11,000 at any one time**. Each tornado could fill an area the size of the USA. Frankly, it's **TERRIFYING** when you think about it too much.

You can see why we have never sent a spacecraft to explore its surface though – it would **BURN UP** before it could get close. We couldn't get within a million miles of the Sun without **bursting** into **FLAMES**.

Lots of spacecraft have explored the Sun from a distance, though, and in 2018, a mission called **Solar Probe Plus** will get almost as close to the Sun as Mercury.

But what IS a star?

A star is a **gigantic** ball of burning gas. Before we ever had a Solar System at all, there was a huge cloud in space of HYDROGEN and HELIUM and the dust left over from old stars, which had burnt out. At some point, this CLOUD collapsed and because of gravity, started to clump together in a dense ball. As it pulled more and more hydrogen in, it started to SPIN *faster* and **FASTER**, and got **heavier** and **heavier,** until eventually there was so much stuff piled on top of this big ball that the hydrogen atoms (the smallest, simplest atoms in the Universe) in the middle began to be **SQUISHED** together to make helium (the second smallest atom). This process releases **huge** amounts of light and heat.

Once that has started, the star just keeps **BURNING** all its hydrogen, turning it all into **HELIUM**. What happens when it runs out of hydrogen depends on the size of the star.

Some stars, smaller than ours, just burn out.

Stars like our Sun are **big enough** and **HOT ENOUGH** that after the hydrogen runs out, the star starts **'burning'** helium instead, that is, **SQUISHING** the helium together to make **EVEN BIGGER ATOMS**. When it runs out of helium it'll leave a huge cloud of those new atoms behind.

The even **HUGER** stars will be even **HOTTER** and after the helium is used up, they will move on to burning the **HEAVIER** atoms, **SQUISHING** them together to make **BIGGER** and more complex atoms, before **EXPLODING** them out across space.

This **EXPLOSION** is called a ...

SUPERNOVA

and it is the **BRIGHTEST**, most **VIOLENT** event in the Universe. We can see them from Earth every few hundred years, like an extra bright star *shining* for a few weeks – although the last supernova we saw with the naked eye was in 1604. We're due one soon.

Basically, **STARS** are the factories that take the hydrogen the **Universe** started with, and by SQUISHING and EXPLODING, squishing and **EXPLODING**, have turned it into all the other elements. **EVERYTHING** around you, (this book, the table, your arm, your Uncle Joe) – its building blocks were made in the core of a star, or in a **SUPERNOVA** explosion. It might be worth taking a moment to look around the room and let that sink in. Everything you see, its **atoms** were made in stars. Then the star exploded and sent the atoms into space. And then they ended up here.

Right, I've got it. What next?

So, now we know a little about the giant **helium factory** that we're **swirling** around in, let's go on a tour of the **planets**. It's a varied bunch, blue, red and green, some with moons, some with rings, SMALL **heavy** ones made of rock in the middle, **HUGE** g a s s y ones out at the edge. Most excitingly, we've managed to get spaceships pretty CLOSE to all of them, which is no mean feat. Take a look at this first one for example …

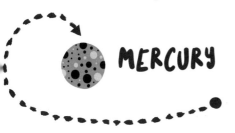

MERCURY

Mercury is the SMALLEST planet in the Solar System, and the CLOSEST to the Sun. It's only slightly bigger than our Moon, and like the Moon it has no atmosphere other than what gets blown at it by the Sun, which means its surface is either incredibly **HOT** (430 °C on the side facing the Sun) or **FREEZING COLD** (-180 °C on the side … well, you can probably guess). It's one of the four terrestrial, or 'rocky', planets in the Solar System and 70 per cent of it is made of **METAL**, so it's got a really **strong** magnetic field …

MERCURY: VERY ATTRACTIVE

Mercury is the *FASTEST* planet around the Sun, but it's historically been a man of mystery — it's the planet we know least about. Until recently, most of what we know about Mercury has been based on data from the Mariner 10 probe, which went there in 1974. The problem is that Mercury is **really, really difficult** to get to. Remember that big dent in space caused by the Sun's gravity? Well, Mercury sits deep, deep in that hole, and you can't just drive up to it and slam on the brakes. You'll just go sliding past into the Sun and that won't end well.

In 2004, NASA sent off the Messenger mission, and to get to Mercury it had to go on an enormously complicated path spinning past other planets, using their gravity like a **slingshot** to first *SPEED* itself up and then to s l o w itself down. It's a bit like slowing somebody down on a swing: if you just stop it abruptly, like, y'know, a wall might, they'll fly off, but if you just take the speed out of it bit-by-bit, pass by pass, they'll have a safe landing. Messenger went once around Earth, twice around Venus and then three times around Mercury until it could settle into orbit. It was so **precise** a path that when they launched from Earth they had all of a twelve-second window to leave. They left on time, and **six and half years later** they got to Mercury.

Messenger has since succeeded in mapping the surface of Mercury, so we now have a much clearer idea of what the planet actually looks like – grey and covered in craters. Another mission to Mercury, with a name like a Spanish detective – **BepiColumbo** – is due to start sending even more detailed information back to Earth in **2025**.

VENUS
6 LIGHT MINUTES FROM THE SUN

Ooh, look at Venus. Isn't it *pretty*? Named after the Roman goddess of **LOVE** it shines more brightly than any star in our night sky. How inviting and **BEAUTIFUL** it is! Come visit me, it seems to say! Enjoy my milky, restful glow!

COME ON OVER ...

DO NOT ACCEPT THE INVITATION.

Venus is horrible. Even though it's not as close to the Sun as Mercury, it's much, much **HOTTER**, (up to 464 °C, even at night!) because it *does* have an atmosphere – a nasty **thick** one, made of **POISONOUS GASES** that would crush you if you went anywhere near it. But if it weren't for the atmosphere, Venus would be quite a lot like Earth. It's made of rock, it's roughly the same distance from the Sun and it's a similar size. There might have been oceans on Venus once, but they have all e v a p o r a t e d. There are volcanoes on Venus, just as there are on Earth, and hurricane-force winds, and rain – except the rain is made of **DEADLY** sulphuric acid instead of water. Venus really **isn't** a very welcoming place.

Exploring Venus: a terrible idea

The surface PRESSURE on Venus is about the same as you'd get a kilometre under the ocean here. So, unsurprisingly, the earliest probes sent to Venus were **CRUSHED** by the atmosphere before they got near the planet's surface. Later missions have been able to send back incredible pictures of Venus, but sending astronauts there seems like a **terrible** idea. The Russians have sent **BALLOONS** in the past to float in the upper atmosphere, above all the acid and the **CRUSHING** and what-not, and that might be a plan NASA will expand on. They have recommended sending astronauts there in the future using **airships**. The mission is called the **H**igh **A**ltitude **V**enus **O**perational **C**oncept, or ...

Acid rain

HAVOC
(not actual airship)

Deadly gas

Tornadoes

HAVOC for short, which is a bit of a **worrying** name.

Venus is nice and **BRIGHT** though, and often it is the first 'star' people see at night. Next time one of your parents sees a bright, low star and says, "Aw, that's nice. I wonder which star that is?" make a point of rolling your eyes and patiently saying **"Actually, that's a planet,"** and then lean in scarily and say, **"And it's the worst place in the Universe."**

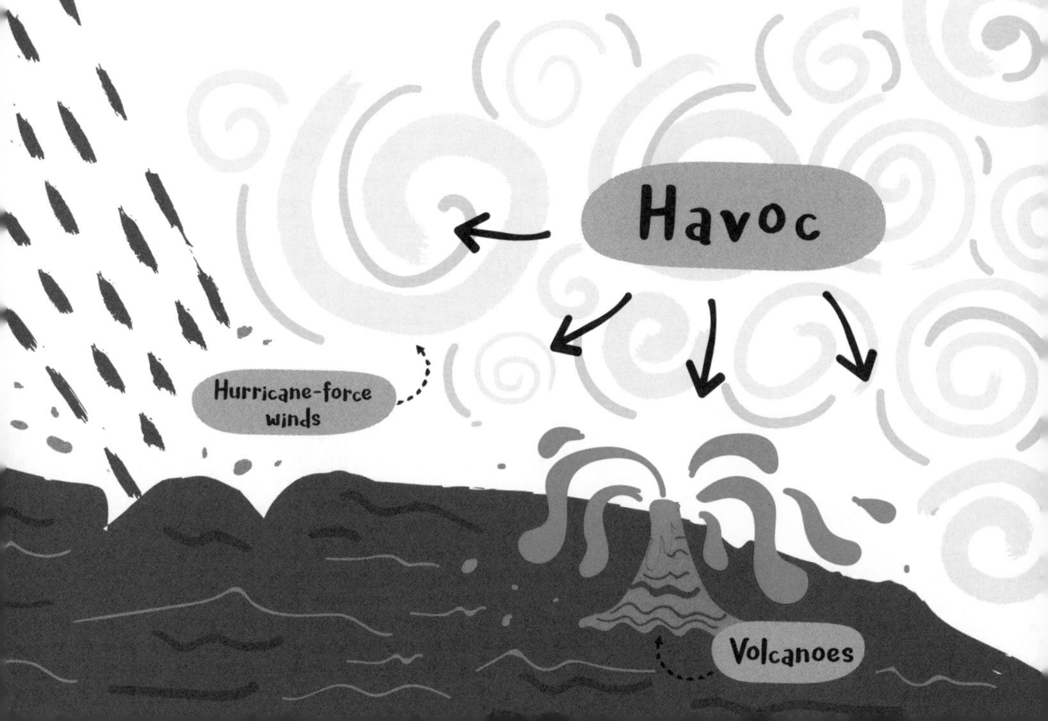

Havoc

Hurricane-force
winds

Volcanoes

The ancient Romans named Mars after their god of war because when you look at Mars from Earth, the planet looks **RED** and a bit **ANGRY**. But that's not Mars's fault – it's the **IRON** minerals in the soil that make it look red. But the Romans didn't have a god of rust, so Mars it is.

Mars is actually the planet in the Solar System that's most like our own. It has an atmosphere, seasons, polar ice caps, volcanoes and even snow. We couldn't breathe in the atmosphere, and it's much colder on Mars than it is on Earth, but that hasn't stopped

generations of people **DREAMING** of moving there if things go badly wrong on Earth.

Is there life on Mars?

In fact, until the middle of the twentieth century, many people thought there was probably life on Mars already. That's why aliens are often called **'Martians'**. Looking up at the planet through a telescope you can see dark patches, which some scientists mistakenly identified as canals built by some kind of gondola-loving alien life form. But when the first successful probe, Mariner 4, studied the planet from 10,000 km (6,214 miles) above its surface, it showed that the planet was **DRY**, **COLD** and **EMPTY**.

UP-AND-COMING
NEIGHBOURHOOD

But that didn't stop scientists sending probes up there to study it. **More than 40** missions to Mars have taken place, and loads more have been planned. NASA has landed four rovers on the planet, all of which look like ADORABLE cartoon robots. The most recent rover, **CURIOSITY**, landed there in 2012. There are no soft landings available on Mars though. Only **50 per cent** of landings attempted there have succeeded. Curiosity burned through the upper atmosphere like normal, then deployed a parachute to slow itself, and then separated into the rover itself and a jet-propelled cradle called the Sky Crane, which gently lowered Curiosity down before crashing itself elsewhere. Had any one of these stages failed, the mission would have failed. But they all worked and to this day Curiosity is still slowly being driven round the surface of Mars.

Inside Curiosity is a **laboratory** that tests Martian soil for the chemical ingredients that make life and that keep things alive: **water, carbon, oxygen, nitrogen, sulphur, hydrogen and phosphorus**. And it has found them all!

Curiosity rover: overachiever →

CURIOSITY and the other Mars rovers have also discovered that Mars was once wetter and hotter than it is now, and that there's still a lot of water underground. So there may well have been life on Mars once – and maybe there still is, deep underground.

A one-way ticket

There are serious plans for future manned missions to Mars. The trouble is, it's not clear how we'd get the astronauts back again.

Do you remember our shopping list from earlier? We forgot to include **FUEL**. To launch yourselves off the surface of Mars for the return journey, you'd either have to carry a huge amount of fuel all the way from Earth, which would make the spaceship too heavy to launch in the first place, or you'd have to make your own fuel on Mars, which no one knows how to do yet. Some people don't mind about coming back, though – plenty have signed up for a trip to Mars with **NO RETURN TICKET**. Crazy human beings and their curiosity and sense of adventure!

Trip to Mars, anyone?

LIVING on Mars would have its plus sides, though. You could take part in lots of **EXTREME** sports, like sand surfing and low-gravity bouncing – gravity is about a third of Earth's, so you'd **BOUNCE** more than twice as high. It would be like living on a massive red bouncy castle. Also, you'd have loads of time to get things done. One Mars day is just over 24 hours, but a year is **687 Earth days**, so the first Mars settlers could invent new months and name them after themselves. If that's not a reason go, I don't know what is.

I shall call it BOBTOBER

Mars also has two moons, **Phobos** and **Deimos**, that are properly TITCHY. So much so that you could probably stand on them and throw something into space; and if you really tried hard enough on Deimos, which is only 15 km long, you possibly, **just possibly,** could jump off it into space. Where you'd go then might be an issue though. After Mars we reach:

THE ASTEROID BELT

(Depending on whether the light is coming from the closest bit of the asteroid belt or the part that's furthest away. The asteroid belt is very big.) Orbiting the Sun between **Mars** and **Jupiter** are **MILLIONS** of massive lumps of rock and ice called **ASTEROIDS**. We think that's where Phobos and Deimos came from, and were then grabbed by Mars to sit in orbit. Asteroids aren't planets, but they can be **HUGE** – anywhere between 10 km to 1,000 km wide. One of them, Ceres, is even classed as a 'dwarf planet', which is just one step below the real thing. The region of space where most of them hang out is known as the '**ASTEROID BELT**'.

The lonely life of an asteroid

When you watch science fiction movies, you sometimes see spaceships flying through an asteroid belt, **DODGING** massive flying rocks. Like most fun things in movies, that's not what it's really like. In reality, the asteroids are as **FAR AWAY** from each other as the Earth is from the Moon. You'd only hit one if you had **TERRIBLE** bad luck and a really, really dodgy steering wheel.

Watch out! There's another one three days away!

While we're unlikely to hit them, they sometimes hit us. Occasionally, an asteroid will get bumped out of the belt – usually because Jupiter's gravity gave it a **KICK** – and start journeying through the Solar System. About once every 1,200 years they'll collide with Earth. An asteroid 45 metres wide just missed colliding with the Earth in 2013. If it had hit, it would have exploded with the force of hundreds of **ATOMIC BOMBS**. Scientists reckon an asteroid probably wiped out the dinosaurs. Let's hope we don't go the same way ...

DEATH OF DINOSAURS

Not ideal

There are nine really **BIG** asteroids in the Asteroid Belt – so big that people used to think they were planets. They have individual names: Hygeia, Iris, Astrea, Pallas, Hebe, Metis, Flora, Juno and Vesta. There's that dwarf planet, Ceres, too, and loads of smaller rocks, but they're just called 'rocks', because scientists don't care about them as much.

Mind you, they cared enough in 2007, when NASA launched the Dawn mission to send a probe to Vesta and Ceres. The Dawn mission was **EXCITING** not just because it was the **first** to ever visit a **DWARF PLANET**, but also because it used a new type of engine, called an **ion engine**. This allowed Dawn to orbit Vesta, map it and photograph it and then, very, very gently, fly to Ceres and orbit that. I know what we all think of when we imagine the engines on space rockets – **huge** jets of **FLAME** and astronauts pinned to their seats from the acceleration. The Saturn V rocket which took Neil Armstrong to the Moon did 0 to 60 mph in 1.5 seconds. The ion engine does 0 to 60 mph in four days. **SOMETIMES IT'S NOT ABOUT SPEED.**

JUPITER
ABOUT 43.2 LIGHT MINUTES FROM THE SUN

Jupiter is **MASSIVE,** stripy and prone to **AGGRESSION**, like a **SPHERICAL TIGER.**

ROAR

It used to be the **bully** of the Solar System — scientists think Jupiter's incredibly strong gravity may have thrown Neptune and Uranus out to the edge of the Solar System, and it may have hurled **ROCKS** and ICE at the inner planets when the Solar System was young. But Jupiter has C A L M E D down in its old age. Now scientists think it helps **PROTECT** the Earth from asteroids — it absorbs them before they reach us — although sometimes it flings them our way, too.

Jupiter is more than twice the size of all the other planets in the Solar System put together, but it used to be four times the size of all the other planets put together – it's constantly shrinking. That's because of the way the planet is structured. Unlike Mercury, Venus, Earth and Mars, which are mostly made of **ROCK**, Jupiter is mostly made of **gas**. The inner layers of hydrogen gas are extremely **HOT**, as is its core, which is probably made of a mix of metal and rock. The planet's outer layer of gases is much **COOLER** though, and the difference in temperature between the hot core and the cool outer atmosphere makes the planet SHRINK – by 2 centimetres every year.

CORE – incredibly hot

MAIN BODY – extremely hot

OUTER SHEATH – hot

OUTER ATMOSPHERE – not very hot

Why so stripy?

Jupiter's stripes and spots are made by the very *FAST* winds that constantly whip across the planet's surface. The reason the winds are so high is that Jupiter spins very quickly – a day is just under ten hours long. The **giant** red spot on its surface is actually a **HURRICANE**, three times the size of Earth, which has been raging for centuries.

It's a good thing there aren't any weather forecasters on Jupiter – they'd have a pretty **BORING JOB**.

Still stormy

Jupiter does have lots of other **EXCITING** weather, though. There's a gas in its atmosphere called methane (it's the gas that makes farts **SMELLY**, but that's not vital to this). If the methane is struck by

But in brighter news ...

lightning, which is plentiful on Jupiter, it'll create a powder of carbon and that will get squeezed by the enormous pressure as it falls. If you compress carbon enough, it makes DIAMONDS. Jupiter is the only planet in the Solar System where it might rain big, SHINY diamonds. Now that is a weather forecast.

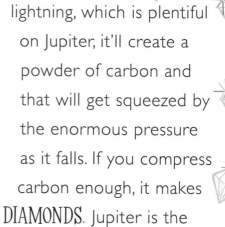

Many moons

Jupiter has a lot of **moons** – at least 67, but there might be more. The four largest – **Io, Ganymede, Callisto and Europa** – were discovered by Galileo in 1610 and totally changed the way people saw the **Universe**. Historically it had always been presumed that Earth was the centre of the Universe, and that everything orbited around our planet. Galileo's discovery backed up the new, controversial **(BUT**

TRUE) theory that the Earth and planets revolved around the Sun. Jupiter might well have a few more moons up its sleeve – we're **DISCOVERING** new things about the planet all the time. For instance, did you know that Jupiter has rings? Well, it does. They were only discovered in 1979, though – they're not as showy as Saturn's.

Europa is also one of our prime candidates for **EXTRA-TERRESTRIAL LIFE**. Not on the surface we think, even at its warmest, it's a nippy -134 °C out there. Plus the radiation from the Sun is enough to kill a human, every day. So it wouldn't be **PERFECT** for us. But the surface is an icy shell (and the SMOOTHEST surface in the Solar System) and this has led to **SPECULATION** that there is an ocean beneath the ice. Just because there's water doesn't mean there is definitely going to be life, **BUT** it was enough to make NASA decide to crash the probe Galileo into Jupiter at the end of its mission, rather than risk it hitting Europa and dropping smelly Earth germs all over whatever aliens might be there.

Obviously, humans haven't visited Jupiter, and probably **NEVER** will. It has the most powerful magnetic field of any planet – 20,000 times as **strong** as Earth's – which sends out **DEADLY** radiation no human could survive. We've sent several missions to Jupiter, though. The latest, **JUNO**, arrived at Jupiter on 4 July 2016, after a journey that took five years, despite it being the fastest man-made object in history. (How many ready-meals to get an astronaut to Jupiter?) It has sent back **INCREDIBLE** pictures of the planet's North Pole and scientists are using it to figure out why the planet's **MAGNETIC** field is so strong. Juno will fly a complex and challenging series of orbits in order to tell us more than we have ever known about this monster of a planet. And then we'll crash it into the surface.

SATURN •
1.3 LIGHT HOURS AWAY FROM THE SUN

As you approach Saturn, the second **LARGEST** planet in the Solar System, it looks silent. **MAJESTIC**. Peaceful. **But it's not.** Being on the planet would be like standing in the middle of a **massive** roundabout, surrounded by vast motorways with no speed limit.

Saturn: in need of a zebra crossing

Ring, ring

Saturn's famous **RINGS** are made of chunks of ice and rock, some as small as pebbles, some as massive as mountains. They are what's left of icy comets, asteroids and moons that were **SUCKED** in by Saturn's gravity and smashed to pieces as they crashed into each other. They race around and around Saturn in rings at different speeds — like **giant** joyriding snowballs, in a rush to get nowhere in particular. Some of the chunks of ice have formed moons. Scientists have discovered up to 62 moons **orbiting** Saturn so far — but there may be more.

Saturn itself, like Jupiter, is made of hydrogen and helium **gas** and, like Jupiter, its stripes are caused by high winds. Saturn is much less dense than Jupiter, though — if there were a **bath** big enough and enough **WATER** to fill it, Saturn would float. It might be worth pausing here just to get our heads around that. Saturn is just a giant rubber duck.

Saturn! Did you leave a dirty ring in the bath again?

A planet far, far away

Saturn is the most DISTANT planet that people in ancient times knew about. When Galileo Galilei looked at Saturn through his TELESCOPE for the first time, he could make out the rings, but his equipment wasn't advanced enough for him to tell **exactly** what they were. He thought they were separate spheres. Later on, he thought they were a bit like **ears** or **handles** on a jug. In 1659, a Dutch astronomer, Christiaan Huygens, figured out Saturn had a ring – he thought there was just one. And in 1675, Italian astronomer Jean-Dominique Cassini realized there was a huge G A P between what are now known as the **A** and **B** rings.

The most recent mission to study Saturn, Cassini-Huygens, is named after these two men. The Huygens probe entered the atmosphere of Titan, Saturn's **LARGEST** moon, and discovered that Titan is a lot like Earth used to be, BILLIONS OF YEARS AGO. The Cassini spacecraft **orbited** Saturn, sending back **INCREDIBLE** pictures and data that led to new discoveries, like the fact that there's a **mysterious hexagon SPINNING** above the planet's North Pole.

Mysterious hexagon →

I would tell you why I'm here, but then I'd have to kill you

Cassini **PLUNGED** into Saturn's atmosphere on purpose in September 2017 and is no longer with us. We really need to find a **NICER** retirement plan for these guys.

URANUS

Uranus has had a **TOUGH** time of it. No one even knew it existed until 1781 – it was the first planet to be discovered with a **TELESCOPE**. **William Herschel**, the astronomer who discovered it, found it hard to convince people it was a new planet rather than a comet or a star. And the man who did get it **OFFICIALLY** recognised as a planet, **Johann Elert Bode**, chose, for some reason, to call it '**URANUS**'. Sure, that's the name of the Roman god of the sky, but the poor planet has been

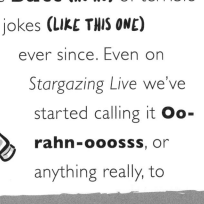

the **butt (HO HO)** of terrible jokes **(LIKE THIS ONE)** ever since. Even on *Stargazing Live* we've started calling it **Oo-rahn-ooosss**, or anything really, to avoid the 'your bum!' jokes. William Herschel wanted to name the planet Georgium Sidus after King George III, which would have been much less embarrassing, even though George III was slightly **mad** and once had a chat with a **TREE**, thinking it was the King of Prussia.

Uranus has **suffered** physically, too. At some point in the distant past, an object the size of the Earth probably **CRASHED** into it and tilted it off centre. Now it orbits the Sun on its side, like a not-very-good break dancer. It **SPINS** from east to west, instead of from west to east like every other planet except Venus. And we know what Venus is like.

← Venus: still horrible

Like Saturn and Jupiter, Uranus has **rings**. It's made of G A S, too — mostly hydrogen and helium, but also some methane, which makes it look blue. Methane absorbs the red light from the Sun and reflects the blue and green light, so it looks blue and green to us. (Although sunlight looks white, it's made up of a whole spectrum of colours, like a RAINBOW.)

Billy no-mates

Poor, **lonely** Uranus has only been visited by one spacecraft and that was more than 30 years ago. It doesn't have a surface for a spaceship to land on, and its atmosphere would **DESTROY** a metal spacecraft. Besides, it takes **years** and **years** for spaceships to reach it. Hopefully we'll visit it again in the future though and find out some more about it.

I'm feeling blue

NEPTUNE
4.1 LIGHT HOURS FROM THE SUN

Maths is useful for all sorts of things — checking you got the right change when you bought a bag of crisps; working out how many days of school you've got left before summer; and **discovering** new planets.

That's right — maths can help you discover planets you can't even see. That's what happened with Neptune, the most

DISTANT

planet in the Solar System. In the 1840s, two rival mathematicians named **Urbain Le Verrier** and **John Couch Adams** separately realized that a **large**, unknown planet was affecting Uranus's orbit — pulling Uranus with its **GRAVITY** — and worked out exactly where it must be. In 1846, astronomer Johann Galle followed up on Le Verrier's prediction and saw

Neptune for the first time through a telescope. He named the planet after the Roman god of the sea because it's BRIGHT BLUE. We don't know why it's so blue yet – we haven't got close enough to find out.

Brrr

Neptune is **very**, **very** far away from the Sun – 4.5 billion km – which means it's **very**, **very** COLD. It has six KNOWN rings and thirteen KNOWN moons. I'm writing 'KNOWN' a lot because there's so much we *don't* KNOW about this planet. We do know that it orbits the Sun once every 165 years. It has only completed ONE orbit of the Sun since it was discovered. If there were living things on Neptune, they'd have to wait an awfully *l o n g* time to celebrate their birthday.

ONE TODAY!

Neptune has only been visited **ONCE**, by the same Voyager 2 that took our **ONLY** photos of Uranus. Put that on your to-do list:

TO DO LIST:

Feed the dog

Clean my room

Do maths homework

Explore Uranus and Neptune!

It's not the **FURTHEST** we've explored though. Although, controversially, the next one is the only time we set off for a planet and when we arrived **it wasn't a planet any more.**

Neptune is the eighth and last planet in the Solar System – as far as we know. When I was growing up, there were **nine** planets, though. The last one was a small, COLD, **LUMP** of rock named PLUTO. It's not named after the cartoon dog, by the way, but the name was chosen in 1930 by an 11 year-old girl, Venetia Burnley from Oxford, after Pluto, the **ROMAN GOD OF THE UNDERWORLD**. The cartoon dog came later. Venetia was given £5 for coming up with the name and Pluto became a sensation. At the time, it was thought that Pluto could be a planet as **huge** as seven Earths. Now, however, it is reckoned to be only 1/459 of Earth's **mass**.

As our most *DISTANT* planet it remained the last great conquest. In 2001, project **New Horizon** started to send a probe to our very *farthest* neighbour. On 19 January 2006, it was launched on its **nine-and-a-half-year** flight. Six months later, with New Horizons already past Mars and well on its way, it was announced that Pluto wasn't a planet after all.

So, what is a planet then?

These are the **RULES** the International Astronomical Union (IAU) decided for what makes a **PLANET**:

1. It has to orbit the Sun.

2. It has to be round or nearly round in shape – so, shaped like a ball.

3. It has to clear the area around its orbit – push other things out of its way with its impressive size and gravity.

Pluto fulfils the first two criteria, but it doesn't have enough gravity to clear things out of its way. So now it's a **dwarf planet**.

Nothing special

Pluto, it turns out, is just one of tens of thousands of FROZEN dwarf planets and asteroids in an area of the Solar System known as the **Kuiper Belt**. The Kuiper Belt is a lot like the Asteroid Belt, but much colder, because it's further from the Sun. It's a bit like a **massive**, ICY pancake.

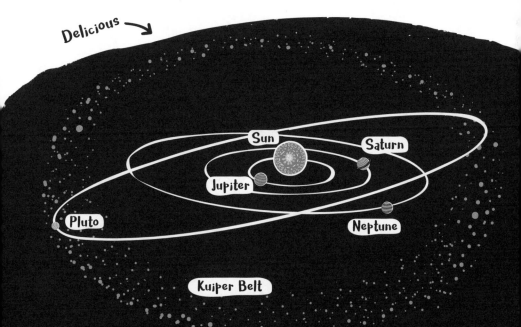

Delicious

Scientists think there are **THOUSANDS** of objects that measure 100 km across in the Kuiper Belt, and **TRILLIONS** of smaller things too. **Pluto** isn't the only dwarf planet out there — so far, four others have been discovered: **Ceres, Haumea, Makemake** and **Eris**.

The Kuiper Belt is named after astronomer **Gerard Kuiper**, the scientist who figured out that the Kuiper Belt must exist, in 1951. His prediction was finally proven by scientists **Jane Luu** and **David Jewitt** in 1992.

CLEVER   +   ALSO CLEVER

New Horizons kept going though, undaunted. So far it's sent back **AMAZING PHOTOS** of Pluto and its moons, including four moons no one knew existed.

Now the spacecraft is flying **DEEPER** into the remote, icy Kuiper Belt, like an extremely BRAVE Arctic explorer, hoping to discover how it – and the rest of the Solar System – evolved.

A new ninth planet?

On 20 January 2016, scientists studying the Kuiper Belt announced that they'd discovered the **MOST EXCITING THING YET**: a whole new planet.

No one has seen '**PLANET NINE**' yet, but it must exist, because its **GRAVITY** is making all sorts of objects loop around the Sun in strange, eccentric orbits. Apparently, Planet Nine is about the size of Neptune and takes between *TEN AND TWENTY THOUSAND YEARS* to orbit the Sun. It hasn't got an official name yet. Since it makes orbits eccentric, I propose **'Goofy'**. WHERE'S MY £5?

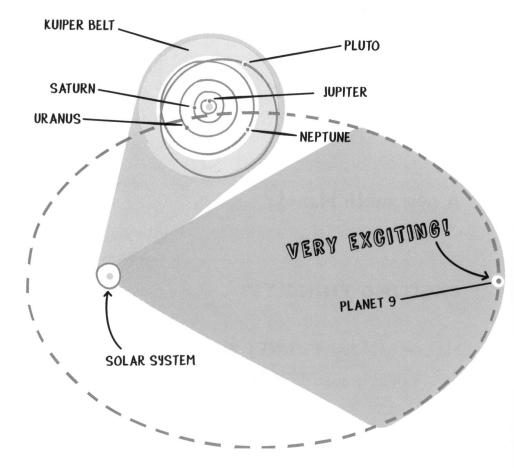

KUIPER BELT

PLUTO

SATURN

JUPITER

URANUS

NEPTUNE

VERY EXCITING!

PLANET 9

SOLAR SYSTEM

COMETS AND THE OORT CLOUD

ABOUT 0.8 LIGHT YEARS FROM THE SUN

Have you ever seen a **SHOOTING STAR**? They aren't very scary. They **FLASH** through the night sky like fireflies and then **DISAPPEAR**. People make wishes when they see them. They're supposed to be **GOOD LUCK**.

Comets, on the other hand, scare the bejeezus out of people. They're like **massive**, terrifying, FIERY shooting stars, and for centuries people believed they were **OMENS OF DOOM**.

In 1664, a COMET appeared in the skies over London. Soon afterwards, a **PLAGUE** epidemic broke out and around **100,000 people** died. Then the Great Fire of London destroyed most of the city. Surely the appearance of the comet shortly beforehand couldn't just have been a **coincidence?**

Yes it could. Shooting stars are just lumps of **rock** and **ICE**, burning up as they enter the Earth's atmosphere. They don't even fly towards us; we fly towards them. Comets leave trails of dust and ice behind them and Earth just **SWEEPS** through those crumbs and we watch the **FIREWORKS** as they burn up.

Comets are just gigantic lumps of frozen gas that travel around the Sun in huge elliptical (rugby ball-shaped) orbits. Comets **GLOW** because the Sun's light warms them up, and their tails are trails of heated **GAS**. Nothing lucky or unlucky about them. Unless one hurtles to Earth and hits you on the head. But that's fairly unlikely. I think comets are **great**. They cheer up the night sky, and if you discover one, it'll be named after you.

OMEN OF DOOM?

FIRE

Hooray for Halley

Edmond Halley: committed to comets

The first person to realize that comets orbit the Sun was an astronomer named **Edmond Halley**. As a child, so the story goes, he looked at the 1664 comet through his dad's telescope (we don't know this for sure, it might just be one of those great stories that stick to famous people in history. Like the time an apple might have fallen on Isaac Newton. Or that time I might have won the Tour de France bicycle race). Whatever the way he started, Halley developed an obsession with stargazing. He studied the night sky for the rest of his life, and went on to make the first **ACCURATE** star map of the southern hemisphere. He also tried to work out what comets were and where they came from.

In 1705, Halley realized that the comets that had appeared in the sky in **1531**, **1607** and **1682** were actually just different appearances of the same comet. He worked out that it orbited the Earth every 76 years and predicted it would reappear in 50 years. It did! Everyone was very impressed, and the comet was named after him. Halley's comet still appears in the night sky every 76 years. It most recently swung by Earth in 1986. **It will next appear in 2061**, when we will all look like this:

Do you want to know my favourite ever of all the space probes we've sent out? It's the one we landed on a comet. **ROSETTA** left Earth in 2004 and ten years later met up with the catchily titled **67P/Churyumov–Gerasimenko**, a **DUCK-SHAPED COMET**, originally from the Kuiper belt, flying at 135,000 km/h on a long orbit around the Sun. Rosetta not only went into orbit around the strange shaped object, but best of all, dropped a lander, **PHILAE**, which was the first human-made craft to ever land on a COMET.

Brave little Philae **BOUNCED** around a little bit on impact, but managed to transmit for a couple of days. They spotted it again the following summer as Rosetta was **orbiting**, but the way it had landed meant the solar panels couldn't get any power. They had to let Philae go to **sleep** on the comet's surface. Rosetta continued to orbit the comet but as 67P travelled away from the Sun, Rosetta was also finding it **DIFFICULT** to power itself. Eventually, after mapping and examining this most **EXOTIC** object for two years, Rosetta's **FINAL** act was to photograph itself coming in to land on 67P, where it and Philae remain,

JOURNEYING through space on the back of the **duck-shaped** comet.

What are you on about?

But why am I going on about comets when we're travelling through the Solar System? Because some comets come from the Kuiper Belt, the ICY PANCAKE orbiting the Sun. An astronomer named **Jaan Oort** realized that some of them must come from even *FURTHER* away than that. In 1950, he predicted that there was an enormous spherical cloud of comets surrounding the Sun, STRETCHING out even further than the Kuiper Belt. And he was right! This **HUGE** region of space was named THE OORT CLOUD in his honour.

If the Kuiper Belt were an ICY PANCAKE, the Oort Cloud

Jaan Oort: he Oort to be more famous

143

would be a swarm of **WASPS** surrounding it. The Sun would be a particularly **SHINY STRAWBERRY** in the middle of the pancake. And the planets would be grains of sugar scattered near the strawberry.

Very serious scientific diagram

The Sun

Kuiper Belt

Oort Cloud

The Oort Cloud surrounds our Solar System, almost like a shell between us and **INTERSTELLAR SPACE,** a place so exciting it can only be written about in capital letters. **INTERSTELLAR SPACE** is the region of space in between stars, far away enough not to be affected by their gravity or energy. It's **very**, **VERY** COLD and **DARK** out there.

From the edge of the Oort Cloud, the Sun just looks like a bright star, but it still exerts a **GRAVITATIONAL** pull on the billions of comets that make up

INTERSTELLAR SPACE

the Oort Cloud, keeping them in orbit. Each comet is about as far from its neighbour as the Earth is from Saturn.

The Oort Cloud is constantly changing. Sometimes the Sun pulls a new comet into its orbit. Sometimes the gravity of another star pulls a comet *out* of its orbit. Sometimes a comet flies off into **INTERSTELLAR SPACE** (still cool), and sometimes it plunges towards the Sun – or Earth. That's how we know the Oort Cloud exists. We can't see it – it's as dark in the Oort Cloud as it is in **INTERSTELLAR SPACE** (okay, I'll stop now).

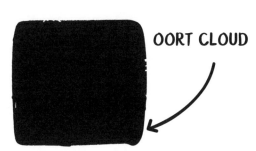

OORT CLOUD

• THE HELIOSPHERE

If you're at the edge of the Oort Cloud, you have passed a really important boundary in the Solar System. The Solar System is **ENCLOSED** in a sort of **magnetic** bubble called the **HELIOSPHERE**, created by winds that spread out from the Sun in every direction at 400 km/s. These winds stretch out until they reach Interstellar Space (there, I've stopped) and then they suddenly slow down, forming a shield between us and the rest of the Universe, protecting us from **dangerous** cosmic rays.

When the solar winds suddenly **S L O W** down at the edge of the heliosphere, they create a **shockwave**.

146

And, in 2014, scientists used this shockwave to confirm something absolutely **INCREDIBLE**: for the first time, an object made by humans has left the Solar System and entered **INTERSTELLAR SPACE** (no, this is amazing again). This object is the **Voyager 1 Probe**. It's currently **20 light hours from Earth**, but it's getting **FURTHER** away all the time.

VOYAGER 1:
AMAZING!

The Voyager space probes: probe-ably the coolest spacecraft in history

It was 20 August **1977**. Your parents were wearing **WIDE-BOTTOMED** trousers and looking ridiculous, if they were alive at all yet. **But what a time to be alive!** There were **no** home computers, or mobile phones. There were a whole **three** television channels and some people were watching them in **BLACK AND WHITE.**

What's on?

Snooker

And yet, there was something truly **AMAZING** for people to watch on the evening news that night ... **the launch of an unmanned, robotic spacecraft named Voyager 2.**

Journey into the unknown

Voyager 2 was embarking on one of the most incredible journeys in the history of spaceflight. Its mission was to **explore** the *furthest* planets of the Solar System, along with its twin spacecraft, **Voyager 1,** which was launched a couple of weeks later, on 5 September 1977. Voyager 1 was called Voyager 1 because it was designed to reach the planets **first**, even though it was launched after Voyager 2, which is quite **confusing**. It probably made sense at the time, **(the 1970s were crazy like that).**

Other things that made sense in the seventies:

LAVA LAMPS

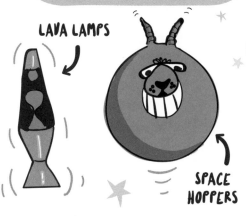

SPACE HOPPERS

THIS HAIRCUT

Many things we loved in the 1970s didn't last very long. This isn't the case with the Voyager spacecraft. They are still sending information back to Earth, over **40 years** after they were launched. And this is after they had already been among the greatest explorers we have ever sent out.

To Jupiter and beyond!

The Voyager probes sent back new information about each of the planets, completely changing what we know about the Solar System. Voyager 1 arrived at Jupiter in 1979 and sent back close-up photographs of the **Great Red Spot** – the **STORM** that's constantly raging on the planet's surface.

Nope, still stormy

When Voyager 1 arrived at Saturn in 1980, it **DISCOVERED** that the planet's rings – and there were loads more of them than anyone realized – are made up of millions of particles of dust and rocks that are constantly **BUMPING** into each other.

So what was Voyager 2 up to?

Voyager 2 visited Jupiter and Saturn too – and then, when Voyager 1 **swung** off towards INTERSTELLAR SPACE, Voyager 2 carried on, visiting Uranus, discovering that the planet has two more **MOONS** than previously thought, and then Neptune, the **FURTHEST** planet from the Sun.

No, I'm not doing that joke

When Voyager 2 reached Neptune, it discovered **six** new moons and a **DARK SPOT** on the planet's surface that turned out to be a **HURRICANE**, like Jupiter's Great Red Spot.

Neptune: another place you shouldn't go on holiday

Journey into INTERSTELLAR SPACE

After visiting the planets, **both** Voyagers kept on going, and **going**, and **going**, like really impressive marathon runners. But unlike marathon runners, who eventually need a bit of a lie down, the Voyager probes will probably keep going **FOREVER**. They might even *exist* forever, L O N G after the Earth is **DESTROYED**. (Which is a bit of a terrifying thought. **But let's not think about that right now**.)

They both have enough power in their fuel cells to keep their instruments going until **2025**. After that, they will continue their journey in silence, through the darkest, coldest regions of the cosmos. They are our **AMBASSADORS THROUGH THE GALAXY**, the only proof of our existence in the emptiest places of all. Voyager 1 will pass the star AC+79 3888 in a brief **40,000 years**. Voyager 2 will pass close to Sirius in **296,000 years**. As they make this journey, we learn just how VAST space really is.

HOW FAR WE'VE SEEN

Voyaging beyond the Voyagers

It's time to **z o o m** out and put this fingerprint we've put on space into context.

The incredible Voyager 1 probe has travelled FURTHER than any other spacecraft has gone before – **BUT** it hasn't actually travelled very far at all. It has only just left the **SOLAR SYSTEM**, and the Solar System is a TINY, TINY part of the **UNIVERSE**. Even if you ignore the Universe and just look at our **GALAXY**, the **MILKY WAY**, our Solar System isn't even large enough to make it on to the map.

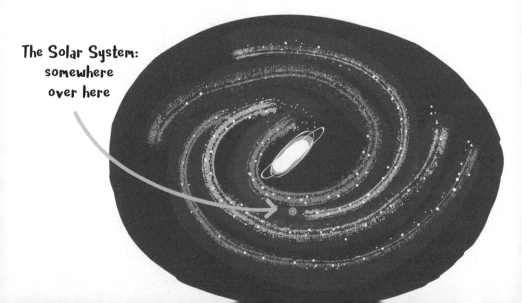

The Solar System: somewhere over here

We're UNLIKELY to ever get a spacecraft to the other side of the Milky Way. As for the Universe in total, well, we don't even know how big that is. It could even go on FOR EVER. We'll just NEVER be able to visit it all. So that must be the end of our exploration then? I mean, we can't go there. How can we possibly keep exploring?

This may be the **greatest** thing about space. If you can't go there, sit back and it will come to you.

Columbus couldn't do that. He couldn't just hire some boats and then sit in Portugal waiting for America to arrive. Scott actually had to TRUDGE across the Antarctic, Livingstone through Africa. They were off getting BITTEN and FROZEN and drowned while you, the space explorer, hardly have to leave your garden. All we've ever had to do to explore the most UNIMAGINABLE landscapes, and then pose the deepest questions about the nature of life itself, was LOOK UP.

Every night, cloud permitting, we have a view out of the **INFINITE** reaches of **SPACE**. We can see stars form and comets pass and galaxies collide. And yes, it might not strike you that this is a very **heroic** form of exploration, or **glamorous**, or **high-tech**. After all, you can do it with a cup of tea in your hands.

But consider this! We will be using one of the **greatest** inventions in the history of humankind, a **TIME MACHINE** that can be stored in the cupboard!

What's that humming noise?

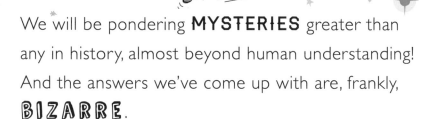

We will be pondering **MYSTERIES** greater than any in history, almost beyond human understanding! And the answers we've come up with are, frankly, BIZARRE.

And throughout history it has required a surprising level of **BRAVERY** to explore this way, and the people who did it, who told us things that seem really obvious now, often ended up in prison, or dead, or **both!**

To find out why stargazing used to be so **DANGEROUS,** we have to take our own journey back through time, to when the FIRST HUMANS started to stare upwards and **wonder** what was happening in the skies above.

Ancient astronomy

When you're looking up at the sky, noticing patterns in the **STARS**, you're being an **ASTRONOMER**. Astronomy – the study of the stars and planets and everything else in the night sky – is the oldest form of science that exists.

The very first astronomers tracked the movement of the **STARS** across the sky so they could mark the passing of the seasons. That way, farmers knew which crops to plant when. **CALENDARS** were created, based on what the stars, Sun and Moon were up to at different points in the year.

Going somewhere nice this month?

Thought I'd wander over to that part of the sky for a bit

Oh, nice – I hear it's lovely at this time of year

We still use a calendar based on the work of ANCIENT ROMAN and GREEK astronomers today. If only they'd come up with a THREE-DAY WEEKEND. That's my only gripe.

And before the invention of **GOOGLE MAPS** – and indeed **non-Google maps** – explorers and sailors used the **STARS** as markers to find their way around. The stars appear to move as the Earth spins, but their **POSITION** in relation to the other **STARS** **never changes** – and you can see them from the middle of the **DESERT**, or the **JUNGLE**, or the **OCEAN**, or a **FIELD** in the middle of Yorkshire, when there's nothing else for **miles** around to help you find your way.

Turn left at the third brightest star on the right

Slightly less usefully, it got a bit mixed up with **ASTROLOGY** and **fortune-telling** for a while, and people thought that your personality could be affected by where the planets were in relation to Earth when you were born. **They were wrong**, of course. When you're born, the **GRAVITATIONAL** pull of a bus passing outside the hospital will have more effect on you than the distant stars.

I see you taking a long journey, as far as the depot

Astronomy isn't unique in having an awkward history like this. **CHEMISTRY**, the science of manipulating atoms and molecules, has its roots in **alchemy,** the **SEMI-MAGICAL** attempt to convert cheap lead into valuable gold. And surgeons, with whom we trust our insides, started out as humble barbers, **not doctors**.

Scissors, please

That's a whole other book though ...

But even though ancient astronomers spent their lives studying the stars, they had no idea what a star really *was*. For hundreds of years, people thought the stars were **'FIXED'**, stuck on a **big**, DECORATIVE wheel that slowly rotated around the Earth, like a TWINKLING CEILING, for us humans to enjoy and navigate by. And since they never changed position, they were regarded as

ETERNAL and unchanging and found themselves at the heart of many religions and beliefs. Created by **gods**, or in honour of the **gods**, or the home of the **gods**, the **UNIVERSE** was ours and we sat right in the middle of it. And you challenged these beliefs at your peril.

A little knowledge is a dangerous thing

Ancient Greek philosopher turned astronomer, **Anaxagoras**, was the first person to suggest that the SUN was a STAR – and that the STARS were FAR-AWAY SUNS – around 450 BC. He ended up in **PRISON**, because his ideas went against the religious teachings of the time.

Another ancient Greek philosopher turned astronomer, **Aristarchus** of Samos, worked out that the Sun was **much B I G G E R** than the Earth (although his measurements weren't at all accurate).

He also figured out that the Earth moved **AROUND** the Sun, rather than the other way around. But he couldn't prove his ideas — the tools he needed didn't exist yet — and he was also threatened with **IMPRISONMENT** for speaking out about his ideas.

Most people **forgot** about Aristarchus of Samos's ideas. Later, another Greek philosopher, **Ptolemy**, came up with a model of the Universe that involved the Sun moving around the Earth. This was what the **CHURCH** was teaching, so everyone felt **EXTREMELY** relieved that no one was about to be put in prison. And even though Ptolemy was fundamentally **wrong** about our Solar System in the most basic way, (he estimated the Sun was only 5 or 6 million km away, and that all the stars were on a sphere, rotating less than 20 times further out) he was still able to create a system to

ACCURATELY predict the **movements** of the planets, predict eclipses and the **POSITIONS** of the stars, a system that was in use for **1,400 years**.

Ptolemy – totally wrong, but he'll get the ships there on time

Then came the brilliant Polish astronomer **Nicholas Copernicus**. In 1543, Copernicus published a book called ***De revolutionibus orbium coelestium*** (say it three times quickly) in which he showed that the Sun, **not the Earth**, was the centre of the solar system. He'd been working on his ideas since the early 1500s, but he waited 'til just before he died to publish his book because he didn't think the Church would take kindly to it. He was correct. The Catholic Church eventually **BANNED** the book –

but not before his ideas had caught the attention of other **SCIENTISTS** and **PHILOSOPHERS**. For the first time in **hundreds** of years, astronomers started to **SERIOUSLY** question Ptolemy's model of the **UNIVERSE**.

When his publishers said it was a deadline, they really meant it

But things got **WORSE** for brave astronomers before they got better. In the sixteenth century, Italian philosopher **Giordano Bruno** said that the Sun was a star, that the Universe was infinitely large, and that it contained many, many worlds. He was **BURNED** at the stake for his beliefs.

And then in 1610, Italian astronomer **Galileo Galilei** looked through the newly invented telescope and realised for sure that Ptolemy's ideas were **WRONG** – he saw moons revolving around Jupiter, so he had **PROOF** that not everything in the Universe revolved around the Earth. Galileo realized that the stars must be incredibly *FAR AWAY*, too. He argued in favour of **Copernicus's** ideas, but that didn't go down well. He was convicted of **HERESY** (disagreeing with Church teachings) in 1633, and was kept under house arrest until he died in 1642. He couldn't even watch interesting astronomy documentaries on Netflix because it hadn't been invented yet. Poor Galileo. He did have a **telescope** though, and he kept **OBSERVING** the night sky and writing about his discoveries until he died.

Can I just go down the shop and buy a Twix? No? I promise I'll come back!

Luckily, the Church **realized** their error eventually and apologised to Galileo. That was in 1992 though, when he had been dead for 350 YEARS.

Hooray for telescopes!

As soon as telescopes were invented, there was no hiding the truth. They **REVOLUTIONIZED** what people knew about the Universe. It was no use locking scientists up when others could look at the night sky through telescopes and see how the Solar System worked for themselves. Between 1609 and 1620, German astronomer **Johannes Kepler** built on the work of **Copernicus** and **Galileo** and for the first time combined **PHYSICS** with **ASTRONOMY** to work out that planets move in elliptical (RUGBY BALL-SHAPED) **ORBITS**. And then **Isaac Newton** worked out what **GRAVITY** was, and that it

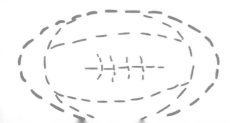

kept the planets moving around the sun. By the end of the seventeenth century, most scientists **AGREED** that the Sun **WAS** the centre of the Solar System, and that the planets revolved around it. And that's mostly thanks to **TELESCOPES**.

YOU'RE WELCOME

This is why the **TELESCOPE** is among the **GREATEST** of all human inventions. At a time when people would do anything rather than admit they were **WRONG**, telescopes allowed the **TRUTH** – that the Sun is the centre of the Solar System – to be seen clearly, until the arguments against it began to look **REALLY STUPID**.

Space may be **AMAZING**, but with the naked eye, it has its limits. Without a telescope, you'll only be able to see 9,096 stars from Earth, all of them in the Milky Way. (An American astronomer named Dorrit Hoffleit spent years

counting them up.) But *with* a telescope, you'll see many more stars than anyone would ever be able to count – **MILLIONS OF THEM**.

If you get the chance, look through a telescope at **night**. You'll be amazed by what you see. The things we are most familiar with become transformed. Even with a cheap telescope, you can zoom in on the **MOON** and see its craters. You might be able to take a closer look at the planets – see Saturn's rings and Jupiter's Great Red Spot with your own eyes – and you'll be able to look out beyond our Solar System to **INTERSTELLAR SPACE** (yep, still exciting).

And if you look through a really **powerful** telescope, you might be able to see right back to the **beginning** of the **Universe**.

This is what I mean about it being a **TIME MACHINE**. Here's how: **LIGHT** is the *FASTEST* thing in the Universe – faster than anything else that exists. It moves at **299,792,458 metres per second**. It's not possible for anything to travel faster than light. But even though light is the fastest thing there is, it isn't infinitely fast – it still takes **TIME** for light to travel. So the light that you see when you look at the stars through your telescope is coming to us from the **PAST**. We saw that when we talked about the Sun being eight light minutes away, and we **joked** that the Sun could have stopped shining seven minutes ago and we wouldn't know it yet.

Well, some stars are so *FAR AWAY* that it takes **years**, or **centuries**, or even **billions** of years for their light to reach us. We can see light from stars that have burned out long ago. We see light from stars that exploded in **SUPERNOVAS** and the news is yet to reach us. We can even see light from stars that died *before the Earth existed*.

Every time we look at a galaxy that is *FAR, FAR AWAY*, we are looking at a **LONG** time ago. It turns out *Star Wars* was **RIGHT** all along.

Telescopes also allow us to do other cool things, like

FIND PLANETS.

PROXIMA CENTAURI
4.2 LIGHT YEARS AWAY

Imagine you've hitched a ride on the FASTEST human vehicle of all time, Apollo 10, whizzing through space at a whopping **39,937 km/h**. You've left the Solar System, and now you're travelling through **INTERSTELLAR SPACE**, which is very **BIG**. You should probably stop off at the nearest star for a drink of water and a bathroom break. The trouble is, the nearest star is 4.2 light years away from our Sun. It would take light, THE FASTEST THING IN THE UNIVERSE, more than *FOUR YEARS* to reach it. It would take you much, **much** longer. Even travelling as fast as any human in history you won't reach Proxima Centauri for *115,000 YEARS*.

How far 'til the bathroom stop?!

Proxima Centauri is a red dwarf star, which means it's **MUCH, MUCH SMALLER** and **COOLER** than the Sun. Its surface temperature is half that of our star, and it's 500 times less bright. Even though Proxima Centauri is our **CLOSEST** star, you can't see it from Earth just using your eyes. If you look at it through a telescope, you'll see what looks like a very **SHINY**, very **ANGRY** spot, or a small **glowing** tomato.

Proxima Centauri also has one **planet** orbiting it (that we know of, there may be more than one). Astronomers in Chile discovered it in **August 2016**, after watching the star for sixty nights in a row, which must have gotten pretty **B O R I N G** by day 47. The astronomers stuck at it though, and **EVENTUALLY** noticed that Proxima Centauri was moving up and down by a metre per second, as if

it was on one end of a seesaw. The question was —
what was on the other end? There aren't any seesaws
in space, or any invisible people to sit on them.
Something **massive** must have been moving
the star with its **GRAVITY**.

Scientists realized
there must be a planet
out there, and they
named it **Proxima B**.

WHEEE

There is a **SURPRISING** amount you can tell about
something that *FAR AWAY* by looking closely, even
when you can't see the thing itself at all, just the
EFFECT it has on its neighbours.

Just from the way Proxima B moves, we know that
its year is **11.2 days long**. It's closer to Proxima
Centauri than Mercury is to the Sun, so you'd think
that it would be incredibly hot there — but Proxima
Centauri is much smaller and colder than the Sun, so

it's actually quite COLD on Proxima B – about **-30 °C.**
It might have an atmosphere like Earth, though, which
would warm things up a bit, and there might even be
liquid water on the surface. And if it has liquid water, it
might have life!

Life on Proxima B would probably be quite **different**
to life on Earth. Even plants would look different.
Because Proxima Centauri is a RED dwarf, it gives out
a lot of RED light. That means any plants growing on
Proxima B might be RED rather than green – or even
BLACK or GREY.

There's no way of knowing for sure, because we can't visit, and we'd all be **DEAD** by the time Apollo 10 got there in AD **117,017**. At the moment, there isn't a spaceship fast enough to travel between the stars.

But Apollo 10 is pretty out of date. It's about time someone came up with a **better**, FASTER, COOLER spacecraft. Don't worry – scientists are on the case. A group of very rich, clever people, including a Russian billionaire (very rich) and the physicist Stephen Hawking (VERY CLEVER), are involved in a project called BREAKTHROUGH STARSHOT, aiming to build a new, fast spaceship that can travel between stars, with a sail that's powered by light. The plan is for it to overtake Voyager 1 (our *FARTHEST* traveller) in four days and get to Proxima Centauri in just **20 years**. But in order for the probe to travel that fast, it will have to weigh just one gram – about the weight of a smartphone chip. You can do a lot with a smartphone … **but you can't travel into space sitting on it.**

The plan is to make the **BREAKTHOUGH STARSHOT** probe gain speed by firing **lasers** at it from Earth. The probe will need to be made out of some super-light, super-heat-resistant material, so that it won't just burst into flames. **What could possibly go wrong?**

But the Breakthrough Starshot team reckon they will actually be able to build the spaceship within the next twenty to thirty years, so interstellar **SPACE EXPLORATION** could be a **REALITY** in our lifetime.

In the meantime, we continue to search for new planets.

We've mentioned **Johannes Kepler** before and he's worth mentioning again, because he was quite **BRILLIANT**. He wasn't just the first person to figure out that planets move in elliptical orbits around the Sun – he was also the first person to figure out how telescopes actually work and the first person to design **GLASSES** for shortsighted and LONGSIGHTED people. He also once wrote a pamphlet for his friend as a New Year's present, called **A New Year's Gift of Hexagonal Snow**, which is probably the best name for a pamphlet ever, in which he described for the first time the hexagonal symmetry of **SNOWFLAKES**.

Johannes Kepler: total dude

NASA named its **Kepler mission** after him – a mission designed to find Earth-like planets in our galaxy. Equipped with a specially designed telescope, Kepler has been watching 150,000 stars for the faint dip in light when a planet travels in front of them. So far it has discovered over **1,250 suitable planets**.

Some of those planets **orbit**, like Earth, in what we called earlier the **'GOLDILOCKS ZONE'**. That is to say, planets that are just the right distance from their star to be **NOT-TOO-WARM** and **NOT-TOO-COLD** for the ideal conditions for life. To narrow it down even more, we can tell if they are **ROCKY** or **GAS** planets, and even what gases might be in a planet's atmosphere, all to find the **PERFECT** candidates.

We might not be able to declare for definite if any of these planets host **LIFE**, and even if they did, we may never be able to communicate with them, but thanks to **Kepler** we've estimated that the **MILKY WAY** is probably home to **BILLIONS** of suitable Earth-like planets, so we should feel a little less alone out there.

❋ ❋ ❋

Probably the things we're most familiar with when we gaze at the stars are the **constellations**, which we've been marvelling at since ANCIENT TIMES. The invention of the telescope, though, suddenly revealed them to be much more than **DOTS** and **PATTERNS**. As an example of the hidden depths of a **constellation**, let's pick one of the most **recognizable** shapes of the **NIGHT SKY**.

ORION

Thousands of years ago, before people knew about the existence of star clusters and galaxies and all that **JAZZ**, stargazers gave names to the patterns that the stars make in the night sky. These patterns are called **CONSTELLATIONS**. The human brain has a peculiar gift for spotting patterns in the seemingly **random**. We also have a gift for storytelling, which is why we named so many constellations after **GODS** and **MONSTERS**, and used them to tell myths and legends.

To be honest, it's a bit like seeing a shape in a cloud and trying to convince someone it looks like a rabbit. Sometimes it works really **well**, like this collection of dots.

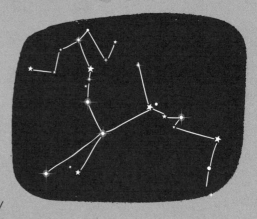

Which does look a little like a **CENTAUR**, or at least a horse, so it became **Centaurus** – the first centaur. Chiron, **KING OF THE CENTAURS**, killed by Heracles with a poisoned arrow!

What about this constellation though? This nondescript triangle of dots is **Leo Minor, the Little Lion**, apparently.

Which is not unlike the triangle of stars that make up **Vulpecula, the Fox**

or the triangle of stars that make up … **Triangulum, the Triangle.**

And by the time they got to **Canis Minor** they'd stopped making an effort at all. **Two dots!** It's hardly a dog. At best, it's one leg of a dog. And not one of the bendy back legs either.

If two dots are enough we could put anything there.

Today, there are **88** official constellations arranged in a patchwork across the sky. The constellations you can see if you live in the NORTHERN HEMISPHERE **(above the equator)** are different from the ones you can see from the SOUTHERN HEMISPHERE **(below the equator)**. And the stars that you see if you live **on** the EQUATOR are different again.

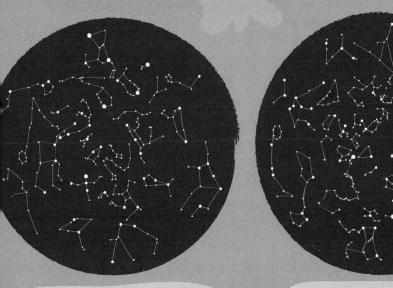

Northern hemisphere

Southern hemisphere

Back when we believed in the **Celestial Sphere** – that the stars were painted on a sphere that span around us – we presumed that the different stars of a constellation sat beside each other, each of them the same distance away from us. Of course, they don't; they're usually many **THOUSANDS** of light years away from each other. It's just pure **LUCK** that they happen to line up like that from where we can see them. Sometimes they are very different stars, much **BIGGER** or OLDER than each other. And sometimes the **BRIGHT SPOT** we see isn't a star at all, but something far more interesting altogether.

Orion is a great example of all of these things, a constellation with **AMAZING** hidden secrets, and so a good one to learn about. In life, it's always impressive to have at least one constellation you can point to, clear your throat and wisely declare, "Well, I think you'll find …". Orion is great for that. For a start, its always one of the most **recognizable** in the sky.

Just look for the belt and the sword hanging beneath it.

Once you've found them, it's easy enough to pick out his **FEET** and **SHOULDERS**, and his raised **ARM** holding a club and his other arm lifting his **TROPHY**. It's a great story, too. Orion was the **SON OF POSEIDON**, the god of the sea. An accomplished **HUNTER,** some say he was killed, surprisingly, by a **SCORPION**. And now the constellation **SCORPIO**, the scorpion, is on the opposite side of the sky, so when it rises, Orion disappears and **HIDES!**

So now you've impressed people with your skills at recognizing a constellation and at your **KNOWLEDGE of GREEK MYTHS**, you can hit them with your **SCIENCE**. The brightest star in the constellation is **Rigel**, Orion's left leg, which is the SEVENTH BRIGHTEST STAR in the night sky. It is **47,000** times **brighter** than our Sun, but 800 light years away and it burns so brightly that it appears **BLUE**.

The god's armpit

The SECOND BRIGHTEST star in the constellation of Orion is **Betelgeuse**, one of the first stars to be spotted and named in ancient times. Betelgeuse isn't the name of a Roman god or anything like that. It's an old **ARABIC WORD** that most likely means 'the hand of the central one', but has sometimes also been more entertainingly translated as '**the armpit of Orion**' so that's the one I'm going with.

There's no **DEODORANT** in space!

You can see Betelgeuse in the night sky for most of the year without using a telescope — it's the ninth brightest star in the sky and it shines with a **reddish glow**. That's because Betelgeuse is a dying star — a red **supergiant**. It's twice as close to us as Rigel (bang goes that Celestial Sphere idea), a mere *430 LIGHT YEARS AWAY.*

As you can probably guess from the 'supergiant' label, Betelgeuse is **huge** — absolutely **ENORMOUS**. It's as big as Mars's orbit around the Sun.

Betelgeuse is nearing the end of its life. At some point in the next million years – possibly as soon as tomorrow – Betelgeuse will **EXPLODE** in a

supernova. It might even have exploded already and we just don't know yet. It will burn incredibly **BRIGHTLY** for a couple of weeks — as bright as the Moon in the night sky — and then it will $\mathbb{DISAPPEAR}$. We won't be harmed, though — we'd have to be within fifty light years of a supernova for it to affect us. It will be an **AMAZING SHOW**, and then poor Orion will have to hold his club for all eternity, with no hand (or no armpit, depending on who you ask).

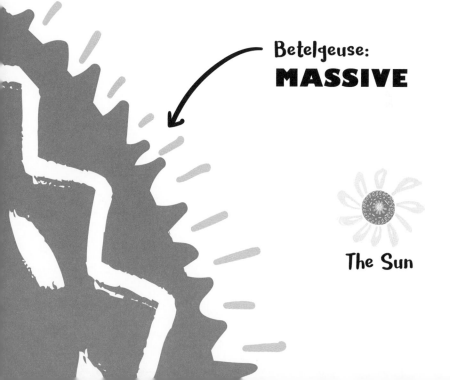

Betelgeuse:
MASSIVE

The Sun

ORION NEBULA
1,344 LIGHT YEARS AWAY

People will already be really impressed with your knowledge of Orion, **BUT THERE'S MORE!**

As we said, if you want to see Orion, look for **three stars in a straight line**. That's Orion's belt. After that, though, look for **three more stars curving down** from the belt – that's the sword.

Orion's Belt

Orion's sword

The **BRIGHTEST** star in Orion's sword, the one in the middle, looks cloudy — as if you're looking at it through a **DIRTY** window, which you might be if your house is anything like mine. This is because the cloudy star isn't actually a star at all! It's **waaaayyy** cooler than that. It's really a **NEBULA** — a hot cloud of gas and dust that forms into stars. The **ORION NEBULA** is our closest star-producing region — a sort of **star-making factory**. The cloud is 24 light years wide, but stretches across hundreds of light-years and is thought to contain hundreds of stars at various stages of development. **EXCITINGLY**, scientists can also see the building blocks of planets, so this region may contain potential systems of **planets** just like our own.

Nearly – just got a couple of red dwarfs to go

Time to clock off?

Orion is also home to the **HORSEHEAD NEBULA**, one of the most famous and photographed objects in space; the Orionid meteor shower, which hits Earth **every October**; and many twin stars circling around each other. But at this stage you've impressed people enough with your knowledge, so maybe time to give somebody else a chance to speak.

Time to go and look at the address we were writing earlier. Do you remember poor old James Brooks of 21 HOPE STREET, BIRMINGHAM, ENGLAND, UK, EUROPE, EARTH, THE SOLAR SYSTEM?

He needs the next few lines on his address just to make sure those birthday cards definitely arrive. The next one is the name of our **Galaxy**, and you've definitely heard of this one, due to it's LIGHT, **whipped NOUGAT** filling.

THE MILKY WAY
30,000 LIGHT YEARS TO THE CENTRE

If you go outside and look up
at the stars in the night sky, you are
looking deep into our **galaxy**, the MILKY WAY.
Every single star you can see with your naked eye is in
the Milky Way. The stars in other galaxies are just too
far away for you to see without a telescope.

The centre of the Milky Way is *30,000 LIGHT YEARS*
away from Earth. The light from the stars you see there
left them around the same time
that Stone Age people were
painting on cave walls.

Graffiti: acceptable
in the Stone Age

When Stone Age people weren't **painting** handprints on caves and **hunting** mammoths to extinction, they probably stared up at the stars in the **MILKY WAY**, too. The ancient Greeks certainly did – the galaxy got its name because ancient Greek astronomers thought it looked liked a puddle of **SPILLED MILK**.

The Milky Way:

there's no use crying over it

We now know that the Milky Way is shaped more like a **gigantic**, glowing **Frisbee** than a puddle of milk. It's about 100,000 light years **ACROSS** and 1,000 light years **THICK**. And if the Milky Way is a Frisbee, then the Sun is a **fly** squished to the edge. Like two-thirds of the galaxies in the **Universe**, the Milky Way is what's known as a **BARRED SPIRAL** galaxy. That means there's a band of stars across the middle of the galaxy and lots of arms spiralling around it. We live in one of the smaller arms – **THE ORION ARM**.

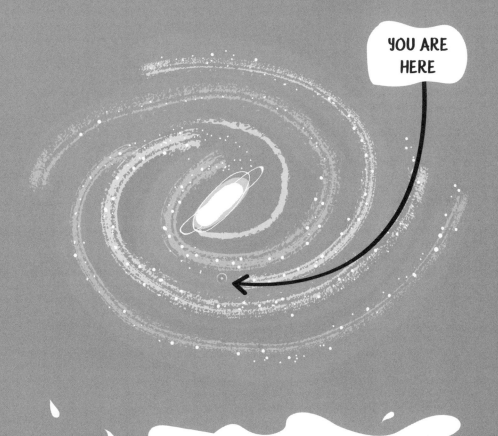

YOU ARE HERE

Like a Frisbee, the Milky Way has a bulge in the middle, called the **Galactic Bulge**. This bulge is so **CRAMMED** with gas and dust that we can't see into the middle of the galaxy at all. But we know that near the core of the Milky Way is a cloud of dust and gas named **Sagittarius B2**, which contains new stars and forming stars. One of the molecules that makes up Sagittarius B2 is **ethyl formate**. On Earth, this is the molecule that gives raspberries their **flavour.** So if you could swallow a bit of Sagittarius B2, it would taste **DELICIOUS**. Unfortunately, it would also **KILL** you, because it contains a deadly chemical called **propyl cyanide**, too. So, y'know, good and bad.

Sagittarius B2: DO NOT EAT

Another thing the Milky Way has in common with a Frisbee is that it **SPINS**. That's why it's shaped like a spiral. It has been spinning since it was born out of a **swirling** cloud of dust and gas formed in the Big Bang about **13.8 billion years ago**. Most of the dust and gas eventually turned into **STARS** and **PLANETS**, but those stars and planets kept on **spinning**, so from above it looks like water draining down a very big plughole.

In a way, the Milky Way actually *is* d r a i n i n g down a plughole. Everything in the Milky Way is getting CLOSER and CLOSER together as it spins, pulled in on itself by **GRAVITY** towards the centre of the galaxy. But it takes over **225 million years** for the Milky Way to complete one full rotation, so it'll take a L O N G time to drain away completely. Because that is sort of what will happen **EVENTUALLY**: the whole Milky Way will D I S A P P E A R into the centre of the **supermassive black hole** at the centre of the galaxy.

Black holes: massive and terrifying

A black hole is an object with so much **GRAVITY** that everything that comes near it falls into it and **NEVER COMES OUT AGAIN** – even light. Do you remember that thing in the museum I kept mentioning earlier when I was talking about gravity – That the coins go **round and round** in? The one a little like the dent gravity makes in space. Well, if it did have a black hole at the middle, there would be no gentle curve. At a certain **point** the hole would just go S T R A I G H T D O W N, and anything past that point, 10p coins, museum curators, light from a torch, would fall down the hole and **NEVER** be able to get out **AGAIN.**

Because light can't escape a black hole, **you can't see it.** There is no trace of it on any telescope. It doesn't sparkle or reflect or twinkle. It just **absorbs** all the light and sits there in **DARKNESS**. The edge of a black hole is called the event horizon. This is the **POINT OF NO RETURN**. If a spaceship crossed the event horizon, not only would it never escape, it would be S T R E T C H E D out, nose first, into a thin piece of string. This is called 'SPAGHETTIFICATION'. Which is a funny name for a really **DESTRUCTIVE** thing.

Worst Italian restaurant EVER

Because NOTHING can ever come out of a black hole, we don't really know what it's like inside. No one has been tempted to go and find out, because of the **being-turned-into-spaghetti** situation. And if you did find out and somehow **SURVIVE**, you'd never be able to come back to tell everyone about it. The Milky Way contains a **few hundred million** SMALLER black holes as well as the supermassive black hole at the centre – BEST TO AVOID THEM IF YOU CAN.

Even a star gets **ripped** to **SHREDS** if it gets TOO CLOSE to a black hole. We know this because astronomers have actually managed to **RECORD** this happening to a star about **2.7 billion light years** from Earth. They've made a video reconstruction to show what's happening to the star. It's **ASTONISHINGLY**

DESTRUCTIVE.

It's like being **KILLED** in both an **EXPLOSION** and being **eaten by a shark** at the **SAME TIME**. Parts of the star falls into the black hole, and part of it shoots back out away from the black hole in an **INCREDIBLY** fast shower of **INCREDIBLY** hot dust and gas that would probably **DESTROY** any planets in its path.

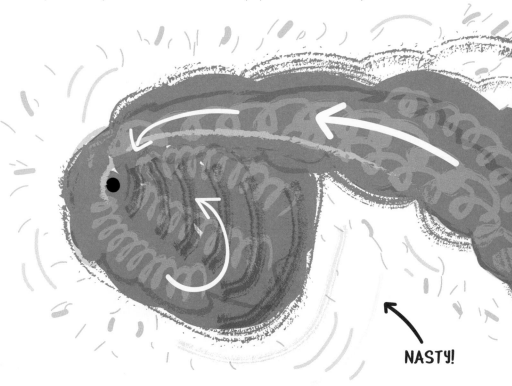

NASTY!

So, even though you can't see a black hole, you can definitely see what it does to the things around it. 'ORDINARY' black holes are made when stars of a certain size (maybe twenty times larger than our Sun) come to the end of their lives. It is the last stage after they have burned all their fuel. The nuclear **EXPLOSIONS** were keeping gravity at bay and when they stop, the mass of the star **COLLAPSES** in on itself into an **INCREDIBLY** dense object, that is, an object with huge mass SQUEEZED into a tiny space. There are also **'supermassive'** black holes which we believe were formed alongside the galaxies and can be as heavy as **FOUR MILLION SUNS**. Scientists think there's a supermassive black hole in the middle of every galaxy, like the Milky Way, pulling all of the stars and planets towards it.

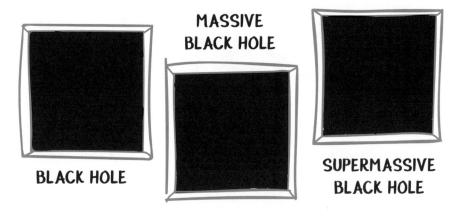

MASSIVE
BLACK HOLE

BLACK HOLE

SUPERMASSIVE
BLACK HOLE

Black holes are the most **DESTRUCTIVE**, mind-blowing things in the Universe and they are, basically, **AWESOME**.

ANDROMEDA

2.5 MILLION LIGHT YEARS AWAY

The NEAREST **major** galaxy to the Milky Way is **ANDROMEDA**. It's a **spiral galaxy** too, and it's 2.6 times as L O N G as our Milky Way.

Andromeda is the **BRIGHTEST** galaxy in the night sky and the most *distant* thing you can see without using a telescope. It looks like a **BLUR** of light, a little bit bigger than a full Moon.

Andromeda is **2.5 million** light years away, and because galaxies are like **massive** Frisbees flying through space, it's getting nearer to us all the time. Andromeda and the Milky Way are travelling towards each other at about **120 km per second**, and in about four billion years, they're going to **COLLIDE**. It's like watching a **s l o w - m o t i o n** car crash that you're powerless to stop.

Galaxies: dangerous drivers

When the Milky Way and Andromeda **CRASH**, lots of new stars will be formed. It'll be great, like a **MASSIVE PARTY!** (Apart from the fact that our Milky Way will be totally destroyed in the **COLLISION**.) It will fuse with Andromeda to form a **super galaxy**. Though it won't be super for any **living things** left out there in our galaxy.

If you've been paying **ATTENTION** you'll remember that our Sun is due to explode and **DESTROY** Earth in five billion years. All in all, things are going to get pretty **EXCITING** in the skies that week.

I've been waiting for this

Do you know when you look at your house on a map on the computer, and look at your street and you press 'ZOOM OUT', and suddenly you're a hundred metres up in the air, looking over the entire street? And then you press it again and you jump back even **HIGHER**, and you can see all the surrounding streets? We're going to do that now a couple of times, to see where the Milky Way fits into the even **bigger** picture. **There's still A LOT more Universe to go ...**

LOCAL GROUP

The Milky Way and Andromeda are just two of the many galaxies in the 'Local Group', a **MASSIVE** cluster of galaxies, **TEN MILLION** light years across. When you look at the light coming from the galaxies in the Local Group, you're looking back to a time before humans – when our ancestors were **APES.**

That's how far away the other galaxies in the cluster are – it takes up to **five million** years for their light to reach us. And yet the cluster is called the **'LOCAL GROUP'** because these are the nearest stars to ours. Imagine how far away the other stars in the Universe are … (REALLY, **REALLY** FAR).

'Great-great-great- ... great Uncle Albert

Laniakea Supercluster

If you were to zoom out far away from the Local Group you'd see that our star cluster is connected to 100,000 other galaxies in a group called the **'Laniakea Supercluster'**.

A supercluster is the biggest structure that we know of in the Universe, but it's really hard to tell where one **SUPERCLUSTER** starts and another begins. In 2014, scientists in Hawaii figured out a new way of mapping superclusters and created the first map of Laniakea, the supercluster we call home. They realized it was a hundred times **BIGGER** than they'd previously thought – 520 million **LIGHT YEARS** across, with the mass of 100 million billion Suns.

520 million light years

The whole cluster revolves around something called the **GREAT ATTRACTOR**, which no one can see, but which must have lots of mass, because it has **LOTS OF GRAVITY.**

The Great Attractor is here ...
roughly ... we think ...

From far away, Laniakea looks like a beating heart, laced with golden arteries and veins. Each vein is a string of galaxies.

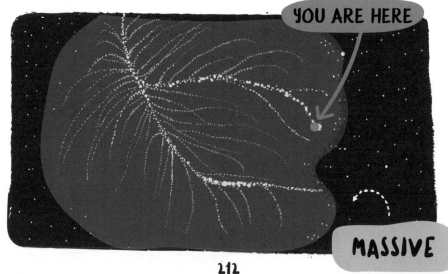

YOU ARE HERE

MASSIVE

Every tiny dot in this picture is a galaxy. It's really hard to get your head around just how **HUGE** it is. That's why the supercluster is named Laniakea – it means 'IMMEASURABLE HEAVEN' in Hawaiian. It was named in honour of the Polynesian explorers who used the stars to find their way across the Pacific Ocean **THOUSANDS OF YEARS AGO.**

But even though Laniakea is **absolutely, mind-bogglingly enormous,** it's just a **TINY, TINY** bit of the Universe.

Tiny, really

GN-z11
13.4 BILLION LIGHT YEARS AWAY

In March 2016, scientists discovered their most **DISTANT GALAXY** yet – and the most distant thing that humans have ever seen. They used the **Hubble Space Telescope** to zoom out past the Ursa Major constellation – and then they just keep on **ZOOMING**, like someone playing around with a new digital camera. Eventually they found a **RED BLOB** that looks like a bit of strawberry jam that someone has spilled in the sky. This **BLOB** is the galaxy GN-z11.

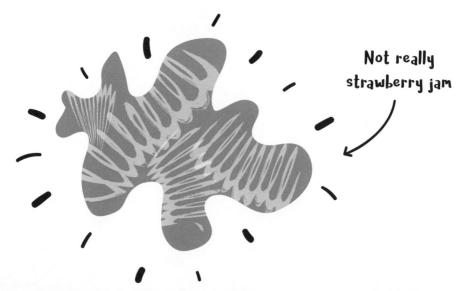

Not really strawberry jam

The light we can see from GN-z11 is 13.4 billion years old. When you look at this galaxy, you are looking **13.4 billion years into the past**.

What was happening on Earth 13.4 billion years ago? Absolutely nothing. Earth **DIDN'T EVEN EXIST YET**, and wouldn't exist for about another 9 billion years. The light we can see from GN-z11 comes from just **400 MILLION YEARS** after the Universe began, when the Universe was basically a **TODDLER**.

When human babies are about two years old, they start **WALKING AND TALKING** and **EXPRESSING** themselves by sticking bits of dried pasta to pieces of paper and calling it **ART**.

A meditation on the transience of human life, by Anna, aged two

When the Universe was a toddler, it started expressing itself **CREATIVELY**, too. Instead of making pasta pictures, it was making the very **First stars**. The really weird thing about GN-z11 is that although we're seeing it as a **BABY GALAXY**, when it had just 1 per cent of the mass of the Milky Way in terms of stars, it's making new stars about *20 TIMES FASTER* than our galaxy does today. It makes the other galaxies look lazy. It's basically a child prodigy.

Redshift at night, astronomer's delight

But how did scientists work out how far away **GN-z11** is? With great difficulty. The Universe is **E X P A N D I N G** all the time, in all directions, so the measurement had to take into account how much the space between us and GN-z11 has **STRETCHED** since light left that galaxy and travelled to ours. And there isn't a tape measure long enough to measure that, so it's all a **BIT DIFFICULT**. Instead, scientists measure the distance using light. Here's how it works:

Imagine a fire engine driving past your house, making that annoying '**NEE NAW**' sound. The siren seems to get higher in pitch as it approaches you and lower when it's moving away from you. That's called the **DOPPLER EFFECT**, and it affects light as well as sound. What's happening is that the W A V E L E N G T H S in the siren are stretching as the fire engine gets further away from you.

EEEE-NAAAAW NEEEE-NAAAAW NEEEE-NAAAAW

E-NAAAAW NEEEE-NAAAAW

EEE-NAAAAW NEEEE-NAAAAW

That makes the sound **DEEPER**. This is what happens to light too – it stretches as our galaxy moves further away from GN-z11, and the **light appears redder**. This is known as **'redshift'**.

Scientists measure how much the light has stretched by measuring how **RED** it is. The higher the redshift, the *further away something is.*

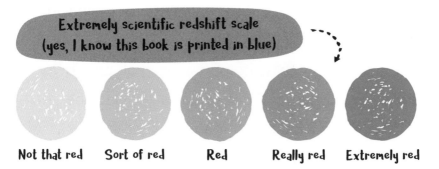

Extremely scientific redshift scale
(yes, I know this book is printed in blue)

Not that red   Sort of red   Red   Really red   Extremely red

Before scientists discovered GN-z11, the highest recorded redshift was from **EGSY8P7**, another galaxy with a name like a **COMPLICATED LOCKER COMBINATION**. The redshift from that galaxy is 8.6, which means it's **13.2 BILLION** light years away. The redshift from GN-z11 is 11.1, which blows the previous record **out of the water.**

Scientists don't think it's possible for the **HUBBLE TELESCOPE** to see any further back in time than GN-z11. But in 2018, a new **TELESCOPE** is going to be launched that will almost certainly find galaxies that are even further away, and even further back in time. It's called the James Webb Space Telescope, and it's named after the man who ran **NASA** when the **Apollo missions** began.

The James Webb Telescope is designed to see **infrared** light — light with longer wavelengths than visible light. That means it'll be able to look through the **CLOUDS**

OF DUST AND GAS that get in the way of other telescopes. It will also contain a 6.5-metre wide mirror, the biggest ever launched into space. Planets will be able to **ADMIRE THEMSELVES** as never before, take selfies with each other, things like that.

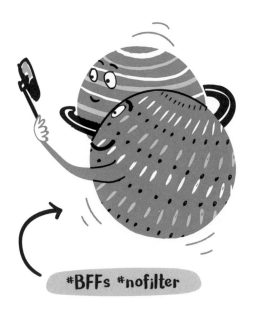

#BFFs #nofilter

It won't be long at all before the James Webb Telescope sends back its first pictures. **WHO KNOWS** what it will help us discover? Maybe half the facts in this **BOOK** will turn out not to be facts at all.

Apologies in advance if that's the case, but there's not much I can do about it. That's just what **telescopes** do to you. One minute you're the **CENTRE OF THE UNIVERSE** and the stars are painted on the ceiling above you, the next, you're **13.4 billion years** into the past looking at the very first galaxies that were ever formed. And the **MORE YOU SEE, THE MORE QUESTIONS** you have, until you find yourself asking the sort of **HUGE** questions that we might never ever get an answer to.

THINGS WE CAN ONLY GUESS ABOUT

PHEW! You just travelled to the very edge of the observable **UNIVERSE!**

Well done, you. We should have a badge printed or something. A special cap, with '**SPACE EXPLORER — GRADE 1!**' written on it. It's certainly a journey that even the greatest minds of a few hundred years ago couldn't have imagined. Poor Ptolemy? He would have **FAINTED** about half a book ago.

He got as far as gravity and his brain just **EXPLODED**

We've **PRETTY MUCH** finished the journey. You could, if you'd like, skip ahead to the **LAST CHAPTER** and read the fun facts that I didn't have room for earlier, then you can casually drop them into conversations to **WOW** people. That would be the perfect ending to a **HUGE**, **EXHAUSTING VOYAGE** to the very **LIMITS OF SPACE**.

I don't know about you, but I'm really TIRED!

But just in case you were interested in a little bit m o r e ...

Firstly, no one will judge you if you find this chapter a bit **technical**, just a bit **STRANGE** or a little more than you need to know. But I couldn't finish the book without mentioning a couple more things, because they are **pretty huge**. We don't have answers to some of these questions or we do have

answers and we're not sure if they're right answers, or we have answers, but we have **NO WAY** of checking if we're correct or not.

These include the questions of how the **Universe** started, how big is it, what is it actually made of and – gulp – **how is it going to end?**

And if some of these answers sound like **GUESSWORK**, well there's **NOTHING WRONG WITH THAT**.

Guessing might sound vague, but done the right way it is actually very **SCIENTIFIC. Newton** was guessing when he said that space travel was possible. He was also guessing when he **POKED** a needle in his eye to see what would happen – not all guesses are good guesses. Giordano Bruno was guessing when he said that the **SUN** was a star and that the Earth was just one of many worlds – he had no way to prove his ideas. And scientists were just guessing when they said there was a planet out past **Uranus**. They couldn't actually **SEE** the planet. They just *worked* out it must exist, because there was something with a lot of **GRAVITY** out there, messing with the planets we could see. All of science starts with an **IDEA**, or a **GUESS**, and then, and this is the **important part**, scientists test out that idea by doing **EXPERIMENTS**. If the experiments don't back up the idea, you have to let it go, no matter how cool it sounds.

Some of the theories in this section **have** been tested and are **probably true** – and some of them can **NEVER** be tested. Let's start with the **HUGE** question.

How did the Universe begin?

Our theory for this must be an **important** one – they named a TV show after it.

THE BIG BANG

The Big Bang theory goes like this: **13.8 BILLION YEARS AGO**, nothing existed. **NOTHING AT ALL**. There wasn't even empty space, because that would have been **SOMETHING**. Time didn't even exist. It must have been quite relaxing, if you could find a chair to relax in, but you couldn't because they didn't exist either.

And then the Universe **EXPLODED** into existence for no apparent reason, in the least relaxing way imaginable.

WITH A BANG

A big one. As the name suggests.

At first, the new Universe was just a TINY **dot**, known as a **'singularity'**, smaller than the full stop at the end of this sentence. That dot contained as much stuff as exists in the whole Universe today. It contained all the matter, all the energy, all the stuff that makes you and me – **ABSOLUTELY EVERYTHING**. It even contained the whole of **SPACE**, and the whole of **TIME**, and all the **FORCES** that bind everything together, like gravity, electricity and magnetism. All of this was SQUEEZED into the tiny **dot**.

It's all in here

After a **hundredth** of a **billionth** of a **trillionth** of a **trillionth** of a second (or in other words, quite quickly), the Universe grew to this size:

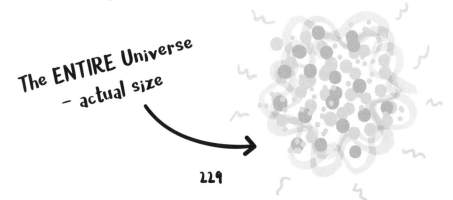

The ENTIRE Universe – actual size

And a few seconds after that, the Universe had **EXPLODED** to the size of a whole **GALAXY**. And it's been getting **BIGGER** ever since.

BIG BANG

EXCITING

We *do* know what the **UNIVERSE** was like when it was a few seconds old: unpleasantly similar to a *BOILING HOT*, pitch-black bowl of soup. And after about three minutes, the earliest kind of matter started to form — tiny things called **'SUBATOMIC PARTICLES'**: protons, electrons, neutrons, photons and neutrinos. After about sixteen minutes, all of the particles of matter that exist today had formed, and were swimming around in a **HOT, SOUPY MESS.**

But atoms, the **BUILDING BLOCKS** that make up everything we can see in the Universe, didn't exist for another **380,000 YEARS**. Before that, the Universe was **TOO HOT** and unstable for anything to exist for long. It was even too hot for light to shine. Light kept being **TRAPPED** by all the **loose electrons** floating around.

And then the soup **COOLED** just enough, and the subatomic particles that had been flying around, too, quickly **SLOWED** down just enough, and **BOOM!** The **first atoms** formed. Light was no longer trapped by loose electrons and there was a **SUDDEN FLASH OF LIGHT**, the remnants of which we still see today.

Cosmic microwave background

The echoes of the Big Bang are known as 'COSMIC MICROWAVE BACKGROUND'.

They were first discovered in 1963 by US astronomers, **Arno Penzias and Robert Wilson**, who were trying to map radio waves from the MILKY WAY. The astronomers were annoyed by a background static noise that seemed to be coming from all directions, at all times of day. They tried **EVERYTHING** to get rid of it, fine-tuning the instruments, cooling them to way below zero with liquid helium. But still the noises persisted. They even thought it might be being caused by nesting pigeons POOING inside their telescope. But they cleaned the telescope out and got rid of the birds, and the noise was **STILL** there. Eventually, having eliminated all other causes, they were left with an **ASTONISHING DISCOVERY**. This crackly static was being caused by **RADIATION** created just after the Big Bang. They were awarded the NOBEL PRIZE for their discovery and the trap that they used to catch the pigeons is now on display at the Smithsonian Institute's National Air and Space Museum in Washington D.C.

Not the creator of the Universe

You can actually **SEE** and **HEAR** the cosmic microwave background for yourself when you turn on a TV set that hasn't been tuned properly. About **one per cent** of that black and white fuzzy static is the **SOUND** of the Universe being **BORN**. It's the sudden burst of light from a Universe only 380,000 years old, still **bouncing** around today.

The most interesting thing you'll see on TV (apart from *Stargazing Live* and *Robot Wars*)

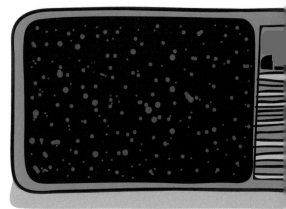

But the Universe realized it had got a bit ahead of itself, **EXCITEMENT-WISE**, and it went dark again for a very, very long time. Nothing existed that could

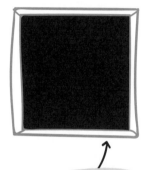

produce light – **no stars**, **no fire**, none of those annoying trainers with lights in the soles. There wasn't anything much to see for a **MILLION YEARS**.

The early days – not much to look at

Then, after about **800 million years**, gravity started to pull things TOGETHER, and the first stars **burst** into life. **THE STELLIFEROUS ERA** – the age of stars – **had begun**.

The **MILKY WAY** formed about **13 billion years ago,** and about 4.6 billion years ago, the **SUN** began to form from the ashes of **DEAD STARS**. Everything we need to live – our planet, OXYGEN, **everything** – is made from DYING STARS.

Luckily the Stelliferous Era hasn't ended yet – **we're right in the MIDDLE of it.** If it had ended, the Sun wouldn't exist any more, and that would be a shame, because we'd all be **DEAD**.

TIME FOR ANOTHER GREAT AND UNANSWERABLE QUESTION:

THE STELLIFEROUS ERA
(much more like it)

What's inside a black hole?

Because time was created at the same time as the Universe, space and time are fundamentally **CONNECTED**. The first person to realize this was the incredible German physicist **Albert Einstein**, who was so famously **CLEVER** that people now use his last name to mean **'someone who is a total genius'**. He was also the first person to realize matter and energy are two forms of the same thing, and that energy could be changed into matter and vice versa. He even created an **EQUATION** to explain the relationships between **matter**, **energy** and the **speed of light** and it's probably one you've seen before.

The idea of $E=mc^2$ is that even a tiny amount of mass contains an enormous amount of energy, since you have to multiply **'m'** (the mass) by not just the speed of light, **'c'** (a really huge number), but by the speed of light **squared**, as in 'c' times 'c' (a REALLY REALLY huge number). We see this if we release the energy contained in mass, in, say, a nuclear explosion.

It's a **REALLY REALLY HUGE EXPLOSION.**

$E=mc^2$ has become one of the most **FAMOUS** equations in the history of equations. Not bad for someone who **FAILED** the entrance exam to college the first time round and whose school report once read, 'EINSTEIN WILL NEVER AMOUNT TO ANYTHING.'

He also demonstrated that nothing could travel faster than the speed of light – not even light that is coming

Still the Universe

from something that's travelling really fast, like the headlights on a speeding car.

WRONG	RIGHT
Albert Einstein will never amount to anything.	Nothing can travel faster than the speed of light

Einstein also had a **FANTASTIC HAIRCUT**, a **WONDERFUL MOUSTACHE**, and he was good at playing the violin. **HE WAS THE BEST**.

Space-time

Anyway, back to space and time. Space has **THREE DIMENSIONS**, that is, three ways you measure it. A **one-dimensional** object is like a line:

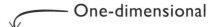
One-dimensional

A **TWO-DIMENSIONAL** object has both length and width, like a drawing of a square:

Two-dimensional

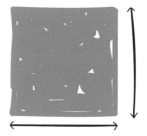

Three-dimensional

The objects in the world around you are **THREE-DIMENSIONAL**. They have depth as well as length and width.

239

But Einstein said that when trying to explain how things work in **SPACE** we need to join these three space **DIMENSIONS** with our **FOURTH DIMENSION**: **TIME**. When you think about it, time is an essential dimension when you're discussing events that take place in space. Imagine you arrange to go to the cinema with your friends at a certain place. You've got the three space dimensions down **PERFECTLY**. However, if you don't also specify the **TIME DIMENSIONS** you'll all turn up for different showings and you'll never meet.

Einstein said that we actually live in a four-dimensional place called **SPACE-TIME**; and it was a bit like a blanket, stretching out into **INFINITY**, a little like this:

Space-time

Matter and **energy** are like balls sitting on the blanket and making it **dip** and **distort**, like this:

Einstein said that gravity is actually a **distortion** in **SPACE-TIME** that's caused by **matter** and **energy**. This is that museum coin-collecting thing I've kept going on about! All this time, **quietly**, you've been studying Einstein's theory of **RELATIVITY!** This is not to be taken lightly. If I'd shown those earlier chapters to **Isaac Newton** he wouldn't have known what we were talking about.

What happened?

Newton read about black holes and fainted on top of Ptolemy

↑ Still the Universe

There are some quite cool things that we get from this. For a start **GRAVITY** doesn't just affect physical things. As well as keeping the planets in **orbit** around the Sun and pulling you towards the ground so you don't **float** up into the air, gravity **distorts time itself**. As an example of this, clocks on satellites travel *FASTER* than clocks on Earth, since the ones on Earth experience more **GRAVITY**. Since we use satellites for things like the GPS in our cars, we have to change the clocks in space all the time, or the whole system would stop working.

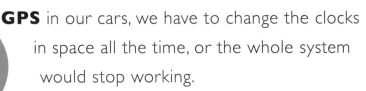

What's got a lot of gravity? A black hole. A black hole is created by a **REALLY, REALLY massive** object, like a dying star, pulling space and time in on itself. At the centre of a black hole, there's so much **mass** – and so much **GRAVITY** – that time and space is completely **distorted**. The usual rules of physics don't apply there. We don't know what it's like in the middle of one, but it's probably really, really **WEIRD**. Some scientists think that if you could **SURVIVE** a trip into a black hole, you might be able to travel to another part of our **UNIVERSE**, through what is called a '**WORMHOLE**' in space, defying the law that nothing travels faster than light. But there's also the possibility you'd just be **CRUSHED** to death, like a bin bag in the back of a bin lorry. But there's **NO WAY** of knowing without actually travelling into a black hole, and there's **NO WAY** of doing that (that we know of) and coming back to tell the tale.

Certain/uncertain death

DON'T BE AFRAID OF THE DARK

The more we looked at the Universe on a **LARGE** scale, the more of a **PUZZLE** emerged. There were galaxies moving in ways that they **SHOULDN'T**.

The **COMA CLUSTER** is a massive collection of galaxies, a bit like our Local Cluster I mentioned in the last chapter. It's about **320 million light years away** so the light we see from the Coma Cluster is from the time when the **FIRST** living creatures on Earth were just leaving the water and beginning to live on land – before mammals, **before the dinosaurs**, before almost everything we know about existed. In other words, if the light from the Coma Cluster were a packet of biscuits, it would be well past its sell-by date by the time it got to us.

Astronomers examining the **COMA CLUSTER** realized the galaxies on the inside were moving *TOO FAST* for them to be held together just by their gravity. Here's why: imagine you have an **open** bag of **SWEETS**, and you get on a roundabout and start **SPINNING**. This is a **BAD IDEA** if you want to **EAT** the sweets, because they'll fly out in all directions, like this:

I did not think this through

That's what the stars in the Coma Cluster should be doing, considering how fast everything is **SPINNING**. They should be shooting out of the cluster, **left, right and centre**. But they're **NOT**, because something **MYSTERIOUS** is pulling them towards the centre

of the cluster. An astronomer called **Fritz Zwicky** observed this for the first time and realized that there must be some kind of MYSTERIOUS **extra mass** coming from somewhere, exerting gravity on the stars. He called the mysterious mass **'DARK MATTER'**. (Actually he called it *dunkle materie*, because he was **SWISS** and spoke **GERMAN**.)

Dark matter has a **GRAVITATION PULL**, but it doesn't interact in any other way with us normal matter types. You can't see it, or feel it or smell it. And there's **LOADS** of it. We now think there's over five times **more DARK MATTER** than 'NORMAL' MATTER. This might not be our Universe at all. All around us is a **HUGER**, **HEAVIER** ghost Universe that we will **NEVER** be able to see.

WE SAY UNIVERSE. BUT IS IT ...

UNIVERSES?

People define the word 'UNIVERSE' in different ways. Some people think it means 'EVERYTHING THAT EXISTS'. But others interpret it to mean 'everything that we KNOW exists'.

We've used the term 'observable Universe' in this book. That's because what we can talk about is limited by what we can **see**; and that might be very, very different to how much is actually out there.

Y'see, we estimate that the Universe is **13.8 BILLION YEARS OLD**. We've worked this out from how fast it's expanding (all that light going red) and just running the clock backwards until we get back to the Big Bang. So we have a nice **SOLID** number for the **AGE** of the Universe! **Yay for us!**

That's one big birthday!

HAPPY
13,800,000,000TH
BIRTHDAY

HOWEVER, this also tells us the **limit** to how far we can see. We can only see something if the light from it **REACHES** our telescopes. That means that only light from galaxies that were, at most, **13.8 billion light years away** from us has had enough time to get here. There may be galaxies *F A R T H E R* away but we have no way of knowing, we're still waiting for the light **FROM** them to get **HERE**.

So, basically we have **NO IDEA** how big the Universe is, but it's a **SAFE** guess it doesn't stop just past that 13.8 billion light year line.

Since we can't see outside of our (OBSERVABLE) Universe there's no reason there shouldn't be **many, many** other **universes** out there. There are lots of theories about what kind of MULTIPLE or PARALLEL universes might exist though, and they're not just dreamed up by science fiction fans bored of waiting for the next series of *Doctor Who* – these are **ACTUAL** possibilities that **ACTUAL** scientists have come up with.

That's a big blanket

Once we realized that the stars weren't actually painted on the ceiling ABOVE US, the question has been whether space just goes on for ever. Some scientists believed that it might be curled up in such a way that it just felt that way; that is, it wasn't infinitely large, but it wouldn't have an **edge**, or BOUNDARY but curve around on itself.

If **SPACE** were CURVED that way, if you could see far enough across the **Universe**, you'd end up seeing the back of your **own** head. It's a bit like travelling around the world – there is no boundary or edge and you could be going for ever **WITHOUT STOPPING**. But we know the Earth **isn't** infinitely large.

The evidence now seems to say that the Universe isn't curved but that it is **FLAT** and NEVER-ENDING, like a massive **PATCHWORK BLANKET**. If it is, you could simply keep travelling forever and **NEVER** get back to the same place. If the Universe *is* just like a massive blanket, then our observable Universe is just a **single square** on that blanket, and you could divide the blanket up into an **INFINITE** number of similar squares, each one of them as large as our **OBSERVABLE UNIVERSE**.

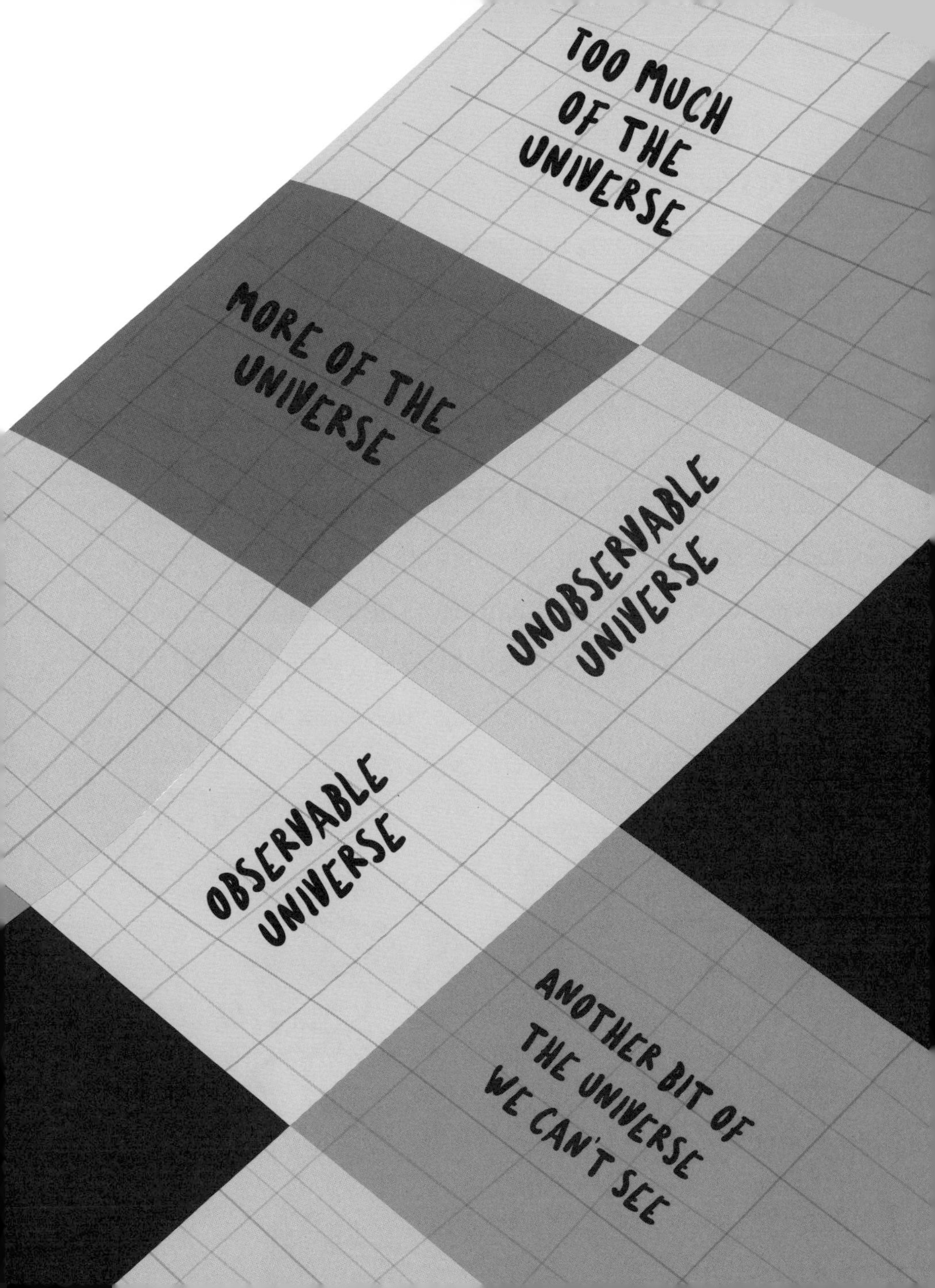

TOO MUCH
OF THE
UNIVERSE

MORE OF THE
UNIVERSE

UNOBSERVABLE
UNIVERSE

OBSERVABLE
UNIVERSE

ANOTHER BIT OF
THE UNIVERSE
WE CAN'T SEE

Here's where this theory starts to get **REALLY INTERESTING**: if the space-time blanket goes on for ever, then at some point the patterns on the squares will **REPEAT** themselves, because there are only so many ways that particles can combine to make things. And that means that there are probably other systems of planets out there that are **EXACTLY** like ours. There could also be **BILLIONS OF EARTHS** that are ALMOST exactly like ours, but with TINY differences, and billions of versions of **YOU** out there. There's an Earth in which everything is like ours except you like **BROCCOLI** rather than hating it for being yuck on a fork. There's a world where you got that exam

Here you go, Bob

Pass the salt, Grandma

Actual scientific scenario

question **RIGHT** instead of **WRONG**, scored that important goal or dyed your hair blue and asked to be called ʻ**JOEY PINEAPPLE-HEAD**ʼ. There could be worlds in which everyone speaks French, and others that are entirely populated by **HIPPOS**, and some where they call everyone ʻGRANDMAʼ except their actual grandmothers, who they call ʻBobʼ. And if there really are infinite universes with infinite differences, then the parallel worlds I've described pretty much **have** to exist. I realize that sounds **INSANE** – deeply, weirdly mad – but it's actually **completely sensible science.**

Bubble universes

But what if there is something *outside* our expanding **balloon** of a Universe? What would that look like? One theory – the **BUBBLE UNIVERSE** theory – says that ours is just one of a series of **ever-expanding** universes, tiny bubbles in an **INFINITE OCEAN** of universes.

BUBBLE UNIVERSE THEORY: appealing to enormous surfers

But what's *outside* the **sea of universes?** Is there some kind of massive beach out there somewhere? Your guess is as good as mine. And yes, I told you this stuff would get weird.

THE END OF THE UNIVERSE

All **GOOD** things must come to an **END, INCLUDING THIS BOOK**.

GOOD THING

All **BAD** things must come to an end, too, **THANK GOODNESS**. You won't have to put up with any more jokes about stars for a while. *Everything* will end at some point, even things that seem to go on for ever, like **car journeys** from London to Edinburgh, **trigonometry lessons**, and the silence after you tell a joke that no one thinks is funny. Even the Universe will come to an end **EVENTUALLY. PROBABLY.** And by this point of the book, you won't be

SURPRISED to hear that no one knows **how** the Universe is going to end. Here are some of the most popular theories about the end of the Universe. Popular among the sort of people that enjoy **HORROR FILMS** based on real-life events, anyway. **None of them sound particularly fun to me.**

The **BIG CRUNCH** theory is sort of the **opposite** of the **BIG BANG THEORY.**

If you think about how the Universe started – as a TINY, **dense** ball of incredibly **HOT** gas – you can see that it has a lot in common with a star. Like the Universe, a star gets **BIGGER** and COLDER as it gets older. Eventually a **really big** star COLLAPSES in on itself because of its own GRAVITY, forming a **BLACK HOLE**.

So, if the Universe is a bit like the biggest star that's ever existed, then it might die the same way that a **GIGANTIC** star dies. There is a lot of gravity in the Universe – PERHAPS one day all of this **GRAVITY** will pull the Universe in on itself and it will collapse in a sort of **MEGA-BLACK HOLE**.

Except **'black hole'** sounds TOO SMALL for how **ENORMOUS** this will be. This will be more of a *'BLACK CRATER'*, or a **'BLACK VOID'**, or a **'black disaster zone that no one will want to go anywhere near'**.

The Big Crunch

Like this, but MUCH BIGGER

This theory is known as the **'BIG CRUNCH'**.

THE BIG BOUNCE

This theory has a nice sort of 'CIRCLE OF LIFE' comfort to it. Essentially, it's an extension of the Big Crunch theory. It says the Big Bang probably occurred when another universe **DIED** in a Big Crunch, and that eventually ours will **IMPLODE** on itself in a Big Crunch too. After that there will be **ANOTHER BIG BANG**, and then **ANOTHER BIG CRUNCH**, and so on and so on, **FOR EVER**.

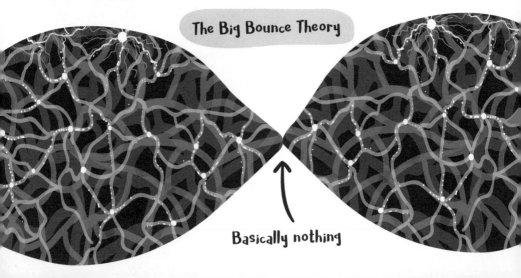

The Big Bounce Theory

Basically nothing

This theory would help to **explain** why the Big Bang happened **in the first place**. Also, we know that NEW STARS are formed out of the **ashes** of old stars – that's how our SUN was formed – so maybe the same is true for universes.

Don't be afraid of the dark, part two

Both these **THEORIES** are based on what would happen if the Universe stopped expanding.

We know that the Universe is EXPANDING, because we can see the way light gets **redder** and **redder** the further it travels. We've worked out that there was a Big Bang that drove the Universe to expand REALLY QUICKLY from a tiny nothing-sized DOT into the vast expanse we have today. Then it all calmed down because all the stuff in the Universe has **mass** and **mass** causes GRAVITY, which pulls things together, right? And now that we think there's a huge load of **EXTRA DARK MATTER** out there, so there should be even more

GRAVITY pulling things **TOGETHER** even more. So how much is the expansion **SLOWING** down?

I'm sorry?

It's expanding faster?!

What happened?

It turns out there's **more** than just us and dark matter in the Universe. We've had a really CLOSE LOOK and something is making space expand **quicker** than it should. We know it can't be more matter, since matter has gravity, so it must be a form of **ENERGY**, and we've called it dark energy. We can't see it, smell it, taste it or interact with it in any way (I feel like I'm repeating myself here ...) and there is **LOADS** of it out there (yep, definitely said this before).

We think the Universe is **67 per cent Dark Energy**, **28 per cent Dark Matter** and just **5 PER CENT NORMAL MATTER.**

Remember that Universe we thought was ours? We're just **ONE TWENTIETH** of it.

Which brings us to the **most likely ending** for the Universe (we think, at the moment), and a much less dramatic one.

THE BIG FREEZE

The Universe has been S P R E A D I N G out and COOLING down ever since the Big Bang, and as far as we know, it's going to keep doing it. **EVENTUALLY**, the Universe might spread out and cool down so much that the stars will **BURN OUT** and there won't be enough energy for new stars to form – or for anything to move at all. The planets will just SLOW to a **STOP**, like balls do eventually when you roll them across the floor. They'll just hang there in space, **completely still**, COMPLETELY SILENT, COMPLETELY COLD. Nothing in the Universe will be left alive. Nothing will happen. Nothing will change. **It'll be rubbish.**

This theory is known as the **HEAT DEATH** of the Universe, or the **Big Freeze**, and it sounds **terrible**.

But actually, seeing as most of the Universe is made up of **dark energy** and **dark matter**, things that we know absolutely nothing about, we might **NEVER** figure out how the Universe will end. Whatever way the Universe does end, it won't happen for at least a **googol years** – that's one followed by a **hundred zeros** – I am personally **EXTREMELY RELIEVED** that I won't be around to see it.

I only hope that somewhere, in a **parallel Universe**, **Joey Pineapple-Head** is having a good time.

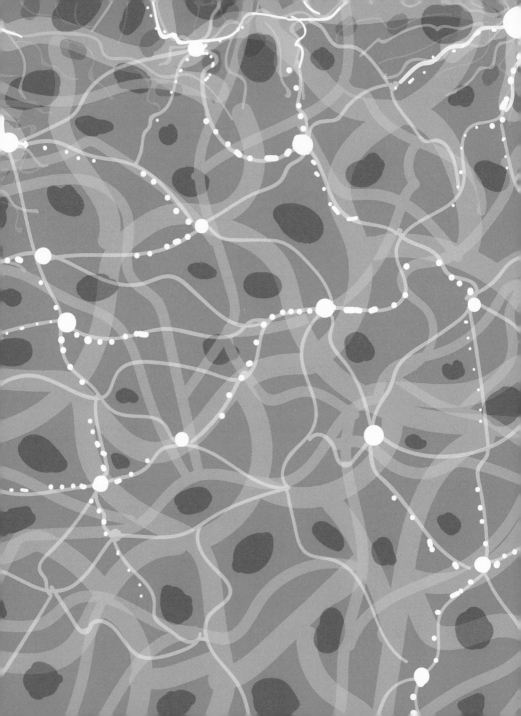

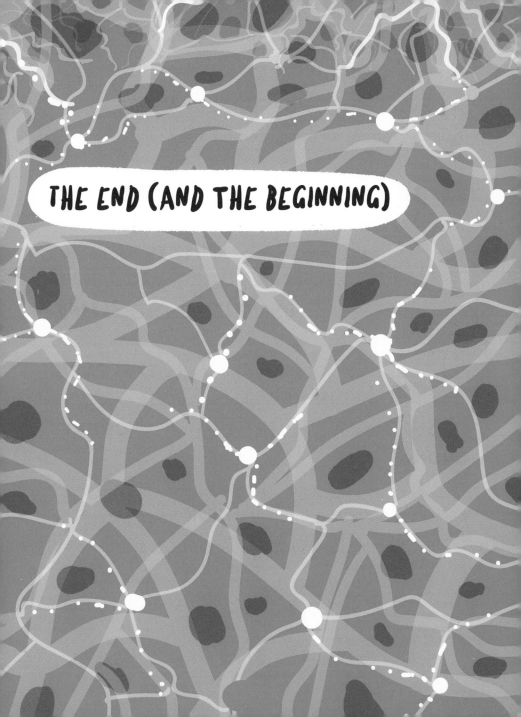

THE END (AND THE BEGINNING)

And **THAT'S THAT**. I think we've travelled enough for one day. You may now **OFFICIALLY SLUMP** in your chair and let out an exhausted breath.

That was a long journey.

We've gone from **CAVEMEN** staring up at the twinkling dots, to the very end of our **UNIVERSE** and then **BEYOND**.

We've travelled from the **EXPLOSIVE BEGINNING** of time and space themselves to the QUIET EMPTINESS of the **GREAT ENDING**.

We've packed our bags for the **MOON**, flown past the great **gas giants** and landed a spaceship on a moving comet.

While we've travelled, we've passed **UNIMAGINABLE BEAUTY** and **WONDER** as stars are forged in huge clouds of interstellar dust **(INTERSTELLAR!)**.

We've seen hideous landscapes, **BRUTAL** and unliveable planets (I'm looking at you, Venus) ... **and I have left SOOO much out.** There really was so much **MORE** to tell you.

DID YOU KNOW that before male Russian astronauts climb aboard their rockets, for **GOOD LUCK** they **WEE** on the tyres of the bus? Even though they are **WEARING** space suits? **FUN FACT:** female Russian astronauts are allowed to pass on this, and bring a jar of wee to pour instead.

Did you not go before we left?

DID YOU KNOW that even though it only takes eight minutes for light to travel from the Sun to Earth, (a journey of 149.6 million km, or 93 million miles), the journey from the **CENTRE** of the Sun to its **SURFACE** takes a **MILLION YEARS?**

The traffic is a bit much!

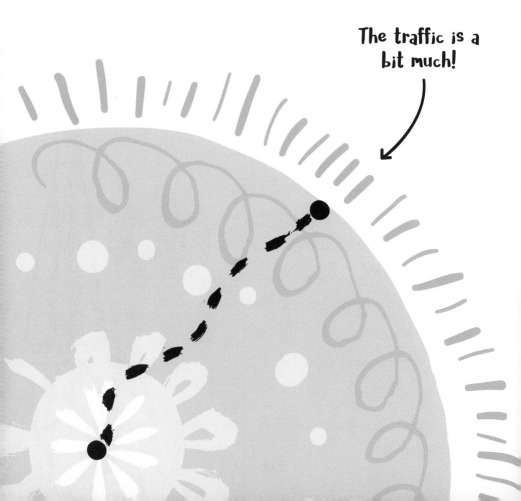

DID YOU KNOW that when **Buzz Aldrin** came home from the Moon, he had to send in an expenses form for a journey he described as 'Houston – Florida – Moon – Pacific Ocean – Texas' and he was given back $33 petrol money?

DID YOU KNOW that the **European country** astronauts always recognized at night was always Belgium, because in Belgium it used to be the law that every road must be LIT AT NIGHT, so as the space station travelled overhead, it was the BRIGHTEST, most DEFINED country?

Oh, there was so much more to tell you.

There's still much more of **SPACE** to explore, so many **CORNERS** of the Solar System to visit, so many more places waiting for our **footsteps**.

You should just take this as the start of your **EXPLORATIONS** of space. We have so much more to learn and we need **more** astronauts, **more** rocket-makers and **more** stargazers.

We **NEED** people who can **fly rockets** and do **SPACEWALKS** and **LAND ON THE MOON**.

We **NEED** people who can **float a balloon over Venus**

... **build a home on Mars**

... and control a robot
on the moons of Jupiter.

We **NEED** somebody to design the rocket that visits Neptune and Uranus.

We **NEED** people to capture the particles of light that have travelled for billions of years, and we need people who will understand what those particles tell us about the story of how it all began.

About the author

DARA Ó BRIAIN

One of the UK and Ireland's **best-loved** comedians and presenters, **Dara Ó Briain** is a **BRILLIANT** new voice in children's books. There is no one smarter or more **HILARIOUS** when it comes to talking about our weird and wonderful **UNIVERSE**.

Scientific notes

INDEX

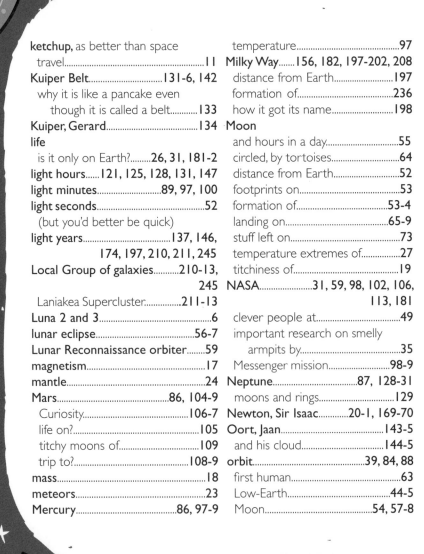